Tehran

This book is an interdisciplinary research work designed to be of interest to a broad range of academics. The book examines the relationship between democracy and the (trans)formations of urban spaces through comparative perspective. It engages with the ideas of "modernity" in architecture and investigates how they might align (or not) with other forms of radical power.

This book offers an understanding of the public spaces through political change, power struggle, and autocratic modernity manifested. It addresses the subject of politics in architecture and built environment by examining the various academic literature in urban studies, architectural history, urban anthropology, urban sociology, cultural geographies, planning history, philosophy, and the broader social and political sciences. Followingly, it will be focused on the less well-known traditions of architecture and democratic values drawing upon western and (non)western perspectives to decolonize the notion of public space in the global south. In better words, the book investigates the mechanisms of power struggles and the transformative dynamism of totalization and state-led modernization, which motivates or shapes a creative tension in the form of the city.

The topic of the work is novel and aims to examine the relationship between the affordances of public spaces, their micro-histories, and the emergence of critical social events and movements. The breadth of the topic demanded engagement with a rich body of architectural theory and history and relevant texts in urban sociology, colonial and postcolonial studies, political geography, and cultural studies, a challenge to which the book has responded outstandingly. The issue is urgent for policymakers and architects, urban designers, political and cultural geographers, and other practitioners working on the built environment to create more democratic public spaces in the global south.

Asma Mehan is an architect, researcher, and educator interested in architectural humanities and critical urban studies. She is an Assistant Professor in the College of Architecture, Texas Tech University (CoA TTU). She was previously awarded four highly selective fellowships and grants, including the Scientific Employment Stimulus Individual fellowship funded by the Portuguese Foundation for Science and Technology (FCT) and the Urban Citizenship Fellowship supported by the Municipality of Amsterdam and the Netherlands Institute for Advanced Study in the Humanities and Social Sciences (NIAS-KNAW) among others.

She achieved her Ph.D. in the "Architecture, History, and Project" program, in October 2017, from the Politecnico di Torino (Italy). Previously, she worked as a senior researcher at various European universities such as the University of Porto, Leiden University, Politecnico di Torino, and Berlin ZK/U center for Art and Urbanistics.

She has taught at TU Delft and Politecnico di Torino and has been invited as the guest lecturer at various institutions including TU Munich, ZK/U Berlin Center for Art and Urbanistics, University of Porto, and Deakin University, Melbourne (Australia). Mehan has received several awards from prestigious institutions such as AESOP, EAHN (European Architectural History Network), Society of Architectural Historians (SAH), ZK/U Center for Art and Urbanistics Berlin, and Society of Architectural Historians of Great Britain (SAHGB).

Her primary research and teaching interests include architectural humanities, critical urban studies, spatial planning, and heritage studies. Asma completed research stays in Australia (Deakin University, Melbourne, 2016–2017) and at the EPFL University, Lausanne, Switzerland (2017), and was a researcher in resident at the ZK/U Zentrum für Kunst und Urbanistik, Berlin, 2019. She is the co-author of the book *Kuala Lumpur: Community, Infrastructure, and Urban Inclusivity* (London: Routledge, 2020).

She has authored over fifty articles and essays in scholarly books and professional journals in multiple languages on critical urban studies, architecture, urban planning, housing, and heritage studies. She has also been a member of several international scientific committees and conferences. Her research reaches academic audiences through international exhibitions, artistic venues, policy toolkits, visual media, journalistic blogs, and online outlets.

Built Environment City Studies

The *Built Environment City Studies* series provides researchers and academics with a detailed look at individual cities through a specific lens. These concise books delve into a case study of an international city, focusing on a key built environment topic. Written by scholars from around the world, the collection provides a library of thorough studies into trends, developments and approaches that affect our cities.

Rio de Janeiro
Urban Expansion and Environment
José L. S. Gámez, Zhongjie Lin and Jeffrey S Nesbit

Kuala Lumpur
Community, Infrastructure and Urban Inclusivity
Marek Kozłowski, Asma Mehan and Krzysztof Nawratek

Glasgow
High-Rise Homes, Estates and Communities in the Post-War Period
Lynn Abrams, Ade Kearns, Barry Hazley and Valerie Wright

Pemba
Spontaneous Living Spaces
Corinna Del Bianco

Vienna
Still a Just City?
Edited by Yuri Kazepov and Roland Verwiebe

For more information about this series, please visit: https://www.routledge.com/Built-Environment-City-Studies/book-series/BECS

Tehran
From Sacred to Radical

Asma Mehan

LONDON AND NEW YORK

First published 2023
by Routledge
4 Park Square, Milton Park, Abingdon, Oxon OX14 4RN

and by Routledge
605 Third Avenue, New York, NY 10158

Routledge is an imprint of the Taylor & Francis Group, an informa business

© 2023 Asma Mehan

The right of Asma Mehan to be identified as author of this work has been asserted in accordance with sections 77 and 78 of the Copyright, Designs and Patents Act 1988.

All rights reserved. No part of this book may be reprinted or reproduced or utilised in any form or by any electronic, mechanical, or other means, now known or hereafter invented, including photocopying and recording, or in any information storage or retrieval system, without permission in writing from the publishers.

Trademark notice: Product or corporate names may be trademarks or registered trademarks, and are used only for identification and explanation without intent to infringe.

British Library Cataloguing-in-Publication Data
A catalogue record for this book is available from the British Library

ISBN: 978-0-367-69190-5 (hbk)
ISBN: 978-0-367-69192-9 (pbk)
ISBN: 978-1-003-14079-5 (ebk)

DOI: 10.4324/9781003140795

Typeset in Times New Roman
by KnowledgeWorks Global Ltd.

Contents

List of Figures and Tables viii
Acknowledgments x

Prologue 1

1 City of Politico-Religious Reasons 7

2 City of Modern Reasons 26

3 City of Power Reasons 53

4 Radical Urbanism 76

5 Insurgent Cities 92

Epilogue 108
Index 113

List of Figures and Tables

Figures

1.1 Heinz Luschey, Negelbert Kaempfer Planographia the palace district of Isfahan. — 10
1.2 Kaempfer's drawing of the maydan of Naghsh-e Jahan (late seventeenth century). As in the illustration, not only did shops surround the maydan, but also its central space accommodated various entertainment and commercial activities. — 13
1.3 Engraving of the Maydan Naghsh-e Jahan in Tavernier. The city square is a positive void as the courtyard of the city. — 18
1.4 Meydan-e Naghsh-e Jahan in Isfahan by Eugène Flandin, 1851. — 21
2.1 Tehran Map (Persian Version), 1852 by Russian Il'ya Nikolaevich Berezin (1818–1896), which is depicted during the reign of Nasser al-Din Shah Qajar (r. 1848–1896). — 32
2.2 Tehran Map 1891 by Abdol-Ghaffar Khan Najmol Molk. — 33
2.3 Oriental Institute founder James Henry Breasted and archaeologist Ernst Herzfeld at Persepolis. — 35
2.4 On Teheran's Streets, two peasants dangle their feet in the muddy waters of a jube (open sewer) and study two Western-clad Bulvardiares who are passing by. — 37
2.5 Tehran 1947. — 38
2.6 The New Map of Tehran in 1933, known as the Street Layout Plan drawn by French Engineer Francois De Romeiser. Black dotted lines show new streets within urban fabric. Red dotted lines show widening of existing streets. — 40

2.7 The plan of new avenues of Tehran in 1937, presents plan of the new grid of streets and emergence of new administrative buildings, in the place of old Arg, close to Bazaar. 45
2.8 The map of existing and proposed streets, 1937. 46
3.1 The vicious circle (up) and the suburban labyrinth (down). 60
3.2 (A) Abstract model of an urban organism: relationship between green areas and urban subunits. (B) Abstract model of an urban organism: public transportation. 61
3.3 Master Plan of Tehran prepared for the Shah of Iran, 1967. 63
3.4 Urban districts proposed by the Tehran Comprehensive Plan. 64
3.5 Ekbatan Residential Complex. 65
3.6 The site of Shahestan Pahlavi is large enough to contain the grand axis of Paris or the entire center of Isfahan. 67
4.1 Tahrir Square (Cairo, 2011), Azadi Square (Tehran, 2009), Taksim Square (Istanbul, 2013–2014), Syntagma Square (Athens, 2010/2012), Puerta del Sol Square (Madrid, 2011–present), Euromaidan or maidan Nezalezhnosti literally means independent Square (Kiev, 2013/14), Palaza de la Catalunya (Barcelona, 2011), Paternoster Square (London, 2011), Martyr's Square or *Maydān ash-Shuhadā,* Previously Saha el khadra Green Square (Tripoli, 2011), Al-Manara Square (Ramallah, 2011), and Pearl Roundabout or Lulu Roundabout (Bahrein, 2011) are some protest squares after 2000. 85
4.2 Azadi Square in Tehran. 87

Tables

2.1 List of streets that were newly built in 1930. The table is translated into English by the author from the original archival document in Persian. 41
2.2 The amount of land as the result of the construction of new streets and thoroughfares starting from 1927 to 1930. The table in translated into English by the author from the original archival document in Persian. 42

Acknowledgments

The following research has initiated in Politecnico di Torino (Torino-Italy) at the Department of Architecture and Design (DAD) and developed at Alfred Deakin Institute (ADI) at Deakin University (Melbourne-Australia). First, I would like to express my deep gratitude to my supervisor Professor Sergio Pace for his support and encouragement over my doctoral years. His consistent assessment and full support show his quality of an excellent mentorship.

I am equally thankful to Dr. Ali Mozaffari at Alfred Deakin Institute (ADI), whose intense and active involvement during my visiting research fellowship in Melbourne engineered the fundamental framework and the backbone of my research. I am lucky to have him as my co-advisor, a fantastic mentor, supervisor, and friend. I am equally thankful to Professor Edoardo Piccoli, associate professor and Ph.D. coordinator of the "Architecture, History and Project" doctoral program at Politecnico di Torino, whose support and generous contribution in developing the research and moving to Australia have been fundamental. I am very grateful to the reviewers—professors Ali Madanipour and Dr. Krzysztof Nawratek—for their valuable comments, advice, and suggestions.

I want to dedicate this book to my beloved family members, my mother Maryam Rezapour Firouzi, my sister Mahla Mehan, and my brother Mahziar Mehan, who are a constant source of inspiration support, and encouragement. I am thankful to my husband, Dr. Sina Mostafavi, for being a continuous motivation and infinite love source. The main credit of my book goes to my father—Masoud Mehan—whose inspiration has been a consistent strength for me. My entire effort has been to make him happy, and he devoted his life to promoting our education even in hard times. However unfortunately, he couldn't see this long journey anymore; however, his inspiring forces and blessings have always surrounded me.

Acknowledgments xi

This work has been extensively benefited from the chance I had as a researcher, educator, and collaborator in the various research centers, universities, and institutions in Iran, Italy, Australia, Germany, Switzerland, Portugal, and the Netherlands; including but not limited to the Art University of Isfahan (AUI), Iranian University of Science and Technology (IUST), Department of Architecture and Design (DAD) and the Future Urban Legacy Lab (F*U*LL) at Politecnico di Torino, Alfred Deakin Institute for Citizenship and Globalisation (ADI) at Deakin University in Melbourne, Australia, CITTA Research Center, Faculty of Engineering (FEUP) at the University of Porto, The Netherlands Institute for Advanced Studies (NIAS-KNAW), Faculty of Architecture and the Built Environment at TU Delft, ZK/U Berlin Center for Art and Urbanistics, EPFL University in Lausanne, Leiden Institute of Cultural Anthropology and Development Sociology (CADS) at the University Leiden, and the Leiden-Delft-Erasmus (LDE) program for Port City Futures (PCF) in South Holland that have allowed me to conduct cutting-edge research in the different Asian and European contexts. I am incredibly thankful to Linda Stagni and Nilofar Rasooli for inviting me to have a fruitful conversation as a spin-off of my forthcoming book at the DocTalks platform in Zurich.

This work could not have been done without the friendly and scholarly support of colleagues, students, supervisors, friends, mentors, and collaborators at these institutions. I am grateful for the support of mentors, supervisors, and professors Jan Willem Duyvendak, Michele Bonino, Filippo De Pieri, Ugo Rossi, Paolo Mellano, Carlo Olmo, Simona Canepa, Matteo Robiglio, Alessandro Armando, Alessandro Coppola, Michela Rosso, Maco Trisciuoglio, Francesca Frassoldati, Francesca Governa, Keith Jacobs, Jeff Malpas, Luisa Bravo, Mostafa Behzadfar, Mohammad Gharipour, Touraj Atabaki, Pamela Karimi, Ashraf M. Salama, Gehan Selim, Doina Petrescu, Robert Bears, Touraj Daryaee, Paulo Pinho, Sara Cruz, Vitor Oliveira, Carola Hein, Sabine Luning, Elena Cogato Lanza, and Klaske Havik. I had the chance to collaborate in research and education with colleagues from various institutions: Marek Kozlowski, Kasia Nawratek, Hassan Bazzazzadeh, Mohsen Ghomesi, Sara Mahdizadeh, Farzad Zamani, Iman Vaghefi, Nanke Verloo, Maria Paolo Repellino, Behzad MalekpourAsl, Aidin Torkameh, Amir Rahdari, Seyedeh Sara Hashemi Safaei, Adam Nadolny, Stephan J. Hauser, Penglin Zhu, Aaron French, Janina Gosseye, Safa Salkhi, Sina Shahab, Rowena Abdul Razak, Bouchra Tafrata, Vanessa Ntinu, Simone Tappert, Giuseppe Resta, Sonja Novak, Mohammad Javad Mahdavinejad,

Lucia Baima, Laura Martini, Eduardo Bruno, Magdalena Janzic, Gihan Karunaratne, Lakshmi Rajendran, Mahsa Alami, Tara Saharan, Neady Oduor, Ahmadreza Hakiminejad, and Chien Lee. In addition to the work, I am grateful for their tremendous kindness and encouragement toward me at different stages of my professional life and career development.

I am extremely thankful to the Routledge editors, Caroline Church and Varun Gopal, and Routledge production team, especially Riya Bhattacharya, for their excellent support and tremendous work.

Prologue

The book *Tehran: From Sacred to Radical* is an interdisciplinary research monograph designed to be of interest to a broad range of academics. The book examines the relationship between democracy and the (trans)formations of urban spaces through comparative analysis. It engages with the ideas of "modernity" in architecture and investigates how they might align (or not) with other forms of radical power. The topic of the work is novel and aims to examine the relationship between affordances of public spaces, their histories, and the emergence of critical social events and movements. The breadth of the topic demanded engagement with a rich body of architectural theory and history and relevant texts in urban sociology, colonial and postcolonial studies, political geography, and cultural studies, a challenge to which the book has responded outstandingly.

The argument starts with the relationship between the political dimension of public space, spatial transformation, and democracy. This book addresses the subject of politics in architecture and built environment by examining the various academic literature in urban studies, architectural history, urban anthropology, urban sociology, cultural geographies, planning history, philosophy, and the broader social and political sciences. Followingly, it will be focused on the less well-known traditions on architecture and democratic values drawing upon western and (non)western perspectives to decolonize the notion of public space in the global south (Nawratek and Mehan 2018, 2020). In better words, the book investigates the mechanisms of power struggles and the transformative dynamism of state-led modernization, which motivates or shapes a creative tension in the form of the city. The issue is of urgent importance for policymakers and architects, urban designers, political and cultural geographers, and other practitioners working on the built environment to create

2 *Prologue*

more democratic public spaces in the global south (Koslowski, Mehan and Nawratek 2021).

The contemporary histography of architecture suggests the critical importance of bringing temporalities, conflicts, tensions, contextual narrations, gender perspectives, and diversity of actors together. However, the new forms of collective narratives, critical milieu, and the role of power relations in architectural analysis are missing. By undertaking the position of an outsider, the philosopher Elizabeth Grosz (2001), in *Architecture from the Outside*, seeks to keep architecture and urbanism open to other disciplines (139). As Steve Basson suggests, architecture is perceived as a continuous and accessible subject of historical knowledge trapped in a linear, chronological order and affiliated organization of forms. Basson questions the linearity of conventional temporality and invites us to let the multiplicity of time spans and disparate discourses come into play. According to Basson (2012), the totalizing vision of convention can be avoided by allowing the multiple encounters, flows of time, and disparate discourses to play in the historical narratives (173–175). For Dana Arnold, the contemporary histography of architecture suppresses the other forms of gender narration and the white western male subject's dominance, which reinforces the masculinist narratives. Arnold (2006) argued that "there is no essential order, meaning or framework as knowledge is forever changing and is subject to periodization or fashion, as is the discipline of history itself" (232).

Similarly, Murray Bookchin argues: "The 'powers-that-be' live in a compulsive fear of remembrance, fear of humanity's social memory of past institutions, cultures, and the search for origins. An essential theme of George Orwell's 1984 is the effort by a highly totalitarian state to eliminate the sense of contrast earlier lifeways imposed as a challenge to existing ones. Thinking itself had to be restructured to exclude this challenge by using words-Orwell's famous 'Newspeak'- that attenuated their previous wealth of meaning and the disquieting alternatives that the past posed to a fixed, eternalized, and ahistorical 'now' or commitment to 'nowness.' Previously, the authority had rested on tradition, often in a highly distorted form; today, it rests on conditioning, with no regard to a troubling past" (Bookchin 1992, 13).

In addition, the lack of scholarly attention to epistemological problems in writing the history of the built environment appeared as the major critique of Eurocentric and Western schools of historiographies. This book analyzes the practices of micro-powers to overcome the meta-narratives (Mehan and Jansen 2020). Following Foucault's biopolitics, "the analysis of micro-powers is not a question of scale, and it is not a question of a sector, it is a question of a point of view" (Foucault, Senellart and Palgrave 2008, 186). The book has its historical sensibilities and links politics and space to respond to this gap. The notion of "politics of space and space as politics" has been employed in urban analysis. Still, this book is setting a new theoretical framework to define the urban projects of the city as the site of political choices, which is a dynamic palimpsest of socio-political inputs.

Rather than focusing on one theory and body of knowledge, the book draws on the diverse readings to highlight the complex interplay of various actors and agencies to highlight the complex interplay of local and global, theoretical, archival, and empirical to "de-assemble" and "re-assemble" the mainstream urban theories and practices. It is only through this free and fair dialectical approach between disciplines that the theorists acknowledge the location and limits of ideas. This book gives us intellectual tools to connect investigations of three different phenomena—built environment, political philosophy, and modern history—but a new theoretical analysis is also an essential outcome of the book.

Architecture and Urbanism in the Global South

The book forms a unique analysis of socio-spatial and political dynamics and urban transformations, focusing on the built environment's political aspects. In addition, to deep historicity, the book engages with a variety of concepts that speak to the questions of democracy but do so broadly enough to cover several major political events or transformations over time.

With the scholarly turn toward the global south as the new epicenter of urbanism, what infuses this book is the explicit commitment to engaging the twenty-first century through a "southern urban" lens, to stimulate the activist, academic, and professional engagement with the city (Kozlowski, Mehan and Nawratek 2020). To account for the questions of how to foster southern theorizing of architecture and urbanism, the new hubs of urbanization, and to investigate the "worlding" of cities, this book aims to outline a different way of doing urban studies. The book engages critically with the more prominent social, historical, and political factors that shape the global development processes in the Global South.

Intrinsic logic (Eigenlogik) starts from the premise that there is something that makes a city tick. A performative understanding of "Eigenlogik" fits into the re-appreciation that took the place of "cultural" factors over the spatial ones. This "Eigenlogik" exists because it is being produced and reproduced by people that explain themselves and others by what is typical of their city. This shows a certain malleability of what is perceived to be characteristics of the "Eigenlogik" of different contexts. Also, it is essential to highlight the continuity and path dependency: actors are limited in their "cultural repertoires" available to their context (Veen and Duyvendak 2021, 27–27). It is important to note that there is a growing interest in this topic because of the rise of protests worldwide, including in other parts of the Middle East region and not only in Iran. Also, there is a lot of interest in urban spaces in urbanism, whether politicized public squares or other sites with cultural and physical attributes that drew citizens to them. Following the Eigenlogik of Middle Eastern cities, this book will continue to generate interest to open new horizons in the interdisciplinary fields of architecture and urbanism in the global south series.

Considering the path-determining issues for the twenty-first century, global south cities are our future. Here, the aim is to celebrate scholarships and flows of thought from the global urban north and south committed to making the urban future diverse, legible, inclusive, and socially just. The southern urbanism scholarship, although not exhaustive or complete, already exists. As Parnell and Oldfield (2014) clarify, "this work on cities from the south, in the third world, beyond the west- however one labels and packages that suite of cities we all recognize by their informality, their diversity, their place, their youth, their poverty, their human energy- is rich" (1). Working from across this multi-sourced and interdisciplinary material, *Tehran* is a contribution to creating the southern urbanism *de novo*. I have configured the chapters to open the intellectual debate, showcasing the diversity of methods, assemblages, timelines and theories, political views, and various research questions.

There is a long-time tendency to overlook the global south cities like Tehran, where traditional authority and religious identity are central to legitimate the new urban narratives in modernization and development policies. This book series gives a more outstanding profile to less-known cities and researches located outside the intellectual heartlands to fill the existing lacuna in understanding the urban practices. *Tehran* aims to inspire confidence in normalizing global south cities like Tehran as common reference points for comparative debate to provide and provoke bodies of work that critically and theoretically inform transformations that come out of the global south. In contrast to eschewing regional or global categorization of a city, where the focus is from a relational, rather than binary notion of south-north-east relations and divisions, the focus here is to reveal the "remigration" and "reverse" the flows of ideas and practices from southern to northern cities, and highlighting too how urban experiences (including the social movements and revolutions) are also global.

The chapters reflect the groundswell of writing on Tehran to connect it to the bigger picture of events, geographies, and most critical contemporary global urban dilemmas. By embracing the divergent disciplinary traditions, this book stands at the crossroad of urban studies, anthropology, development studies, sociology, planning, architecture, and history. This book intends to provide this cohort with an authoritative overview of this rapidly developing subfield of urban studies, known clumsily as Iranian or Middle Eastern Urbanism. The first chapter of the book seeks to open up the discussion rather than take a position on the precise meanings, timeframes, and actors of urbanism in Tehran. This (re)framing challenges the intellectual status quo and makes way for new modes to illuminate the drivers of urban change.

The final chapter of the book aims to theorize the radical urbanization in ways that make transparent how specific local problems resonate with universal challenges, including but not limited to new social media, digitalization, climate change crisis, Global Sustainable Development Goals (SDGs), uneven distribution of wealth, and the political tensions to analyze how much the urban theory has global application. The recent COVID-19 showed the urgent need for multiple genealogies of knowledge production and diversity of empirical entry points essential for excavating the rapidly shifting post-COVID urbanism around the globe. The book ends by looking back and looking forward to post-pandemic urbanism, as this is fertile terrain, and there is much to be done. Focusing on the contemporary challenges, the book's two final chapters suggest thinking about pathways across conventional terrain of north and south or west and east.

The proposed audience of this book is all postgraduate students and academics, within disciplines related to the built environment, in particular architecture and urban history, spatial planning, anthropology, political geography, urban and regional studies, urban sociology, and the Middle Eastern, Asian, and Global South Studies. Since the book is about an approach as much as it is about a particular topic, it will appeal to an international audience of scholars interested in the interdisciplinary study of the city and urban culture, including specialists in urban studies, theoretically-oriented sociologists or urban geographers, architectural historians and scholars in cultural studies.

Note on the Transliteration System

I have deliberately minimized the usual transliteration acrobatics. Preference is given to Persian pronunciation of words, expressions, and names with a few editions, adjusts, modifications, and revisions. I have not used diacritical marks unless the proper pronunciation of the term bears significantly on the discussion. City names in common usage, remain unchanged. As much as I have tried, I am certain there are inconsistencies, maybe even egregious ones, for which I beg the reader's indulgence.

References

Arnold, Dana. 2006. "Beyond a Boundary: Towards an Architectural History of the Non-East." In *Rethinking Architectural Histography*, by Daana Arnold, Elvan Altan Ergut and Belgin Turan Özkaya. New York: Routledge.
Basson, Steve. 2012. "Temporal Flows." In *Architecture in the Space of Flows*, by Andrew Ballantyne and Chris L. Smith. New York: Routledge.
Bookchin, Murray. 1992. *Urbanization Without Cities: The Rise and Decline of Citizenship*. Montreal/New York: Black Rose Books.
Foucault, Michel, Michel Senellart, and Connect Palgrave. 2008. *The Bith of Biopolitics: Lectures at the College De France, 1978–1979*. New York: Palgrave Macmillan.
Grosz, Elizabeth. 2001. *Architecture from the Outside: Essays on Virtual and Real Spaces*. Cambridge: MIT Press.
Kozlowski, Marek, Asma Mehan, and Krzysztof Nawratek. 2020. *Kuala Lumpur: Community, Infrastructure and Urban Inclusivity*, 1st Edition. London: Routledge.
—. 2021. "Transformation of Malaysian Cities: from Colonial Cities to the Products of Neoliberal Globalisation." *The Architect Magazine*: 226–233.
Mehan, Asma, and Maurice Jansen. 2020. "Beirut Blast: A Port City in Crisis." *The Port City Futures Blog*. Leiden. Delft. Erasmus (LDE) Initiative.
Nawratek, Krzysztof, and Asma Mehan. 2018. "Producing Public Space under the Gaze of Allah: Hetrosexual Muslims Dating in Kuala Lumpur." Cardiff University, UK: RGS-IBG Annual International Conference 2018.
—. 2020. "De-Colonising Public Spaces in Malysia. Dating in Kuala Lumpur." *Cultural Geographies* 27 (2): 1–15.
Parnell, Susan, and Sophie Oldfield. 2014. *The Routledge Handbook on Cities of the Global South*. London and New York: Routledge.
Veen, Menno van der, and Jan Wilem Duyvendak. 2021. *Participate: Portraits of Cities and Citizens*. Rotterdam: nai010 publishers.

1 City of Politico-Religious Reasons

Square as Politico-Religious Order in the Ideogram of the City

In 1982, the literary critic Roland Barthes in his book—*Empire of Signs*—represented the squares as the spatial-political orders in the ideogram of the city. Barthes in *Empire of Signs* offers mediation and specific re-reading on Japan's society, art, literature, culture, and language. In his book, Barthes believes that Orient and Occident cannot take as "realities" to be compared and contrasted historically, politically, and culturally. Barthes (1989) added:

> Tokyo can be known only by an activity of an ethnographic kind: you must orient yourself in it not by the book, by address, but by walking, by sight, by habit, by experience.
>
> (36)

Through the case of Tokyo's public spaces, Barthes (1989) offers a precious and continuous paradox:

> It does possess a center, but this center is empty. The entire city turns around a site both forbidden and indifferent, inhabited by an emperor who is never seen, which is to say, literally, by no one knows who.
>
> (30)

Unlike the western tradition of public, often post-secular, hardscaped square, the Japanese, like the Asian and Middle Eastern cultures, have a tradition of public spaces associated with religion, culture, societal relations, and power. Similarly, architectural historian,

DOI: 10.4324/9781003140795-2

8 *City of Politico-Religious Reasons*

Jinnai Hidenobu, in the book, *Tokyo: A Spatial Anthropology*, describes the public spaces in Tokyo as lucid spaces which are not fixed but associated with temporary and animated situations which are deliberately or accidentally fabricated by ephemeral occurrences. These lucid spaces are multifaceted (Hidenobu 1995, 71). In another definition, Shun Kanda uses the term *hiroba*, which translates as "open, or vast space or ground," associated with the place of human activity hinged more to time rather than fixed spaces (Kanda 1974, 85–86). In the absence of actual squares in Japan, the traditional *hiroba* was the human-scale spaces traditionally fashioned warm and renewable materials for the community interactions. Japanese *hiroba* can be understood as the dynamic nonphysical process which emerges by *hiroba-ing* through the spontaneous citizen action, especially during the festivals and temporarily transformation of space into a vast meeting node open to all citizens. In the Japanese context, the meaning of the sacred space is associated with "deepness" or "space with depth" by introducing the concept of *Oku*, known as subjective depth. Following this definition, unlike the western tradition and Eurocentric perspective, the word "sacred" in this book is associated with religion, culture, societal relations with a specific focus on Middle Eastern Cities.

In the 1940s and 1950s, Japanese architects like Kenzo Tange began to develop terminologies such as "communication space," based on studies of the Greek "agora" or Italian "piazza," attempting to fill a void in the Asian architectural vocabulary. In his book, *The City Squares*, Michael Webb traces the Square's chronological, cultural, and morphological evolution from its classical origins to the modern time as the building block of the new towns. Through the illustrated historical survey, Webb introduced the Square as a symbol of authority and the seed the city would grow. Webb represented the new world as a "blank slate" or "blank canvas" on which people had the opportunity and duty to God and Empire to write (Webb 1990, 104).

This chapter aims not to merely consider the Iranian squares as the geographical setting where history happens but rather as phenomena to be understood due to their continuity across the centuries. The structure of the chapter revolves around the central concept of Square as the microcosms of the city (Mehan 2016a). To introduce the squares as the politico-religious order in the ideogram of the city, this chapter enables a possibility of recalling the cognitive, symbolic, and cultural relationship between urban form, ideogram of the city, and main archetypes and paradigms attached to cities that have not been mentioned before in the modern city project.

Meidan

Events during February 2014 in Kyiv, which continues to the 2022 devastating Russian invasion of Ukraine, also put forward a particular word: Maidan or in Russian (майдан) with the same pronunciation. Kyiv's central square, Maidan Nezalezhnosti (literally: Independence Square), became the focal node of riots and protests known as the "Maidan Uprising." The Ukrainian director *Sergei Loznitsa's* 2014 documentary film, *Maidan*, captures the Ukrainian revolution's events over three months on location on Kyiv's Maidan Nezalezhnosti to depict the life of the Occupy Square movement to the confrontation with the armed governmental police.

Maidan is a Ukrainian word for open space, ultimately from the Arabic language maidan, via Turku-Persian transmission, Persian Meidan means "field, park, open space, square." In the Oxford Dictionary of Architecture, the word Maidan (also written as Maydan) has been associated with three definitions: (1) open space in or just outside an Indian or Central Asian town, used for ceremonial occasions, parades, etc., (2) esplanade: the level walk laid out with planting by a river, lake, or seashore, and (3) market-place (Stevenes and Wilson 2015). In its most common functional definition, Meidan denoted a public space of social interaction, primarily to accommodate the need for temporary or daily markets and as a place to showcase the conduct of justice (grants of privilege and public executions) (Babaie and Grigor 2015) (Figure 1.1).

In his book, *The City Squares*, Michael Webb argues that traditional square has been shaped by commerce and defense, political systems and cultural traditions, climate, and topography (Webb 1990, 20). Meidan represented a unified composition at the command of one ruler, which described in *Temple Mount* of *Jerusalem* as one of the holiest and oldest urban spaces that have evolved and expanded over three millennia (Webb 1990, 25–27). Thus, re-reading the square in the city's project leads us to the inescapable logic of Greek Agora and Italian Piazza to *Tiananmen Square* in *Beijing* in 1989 and the recent square movements around the world. Tiananmen Square is so remarkable because it has brought a distinctly politicized meaning to the Chinese public squares, which was unprecedented. The vast plaza was designed primarily due to its unique form and function along the imperial axis as symbolic conservation of Mao's legitimacy (Webb 1990, 177–178). The post-Tiananmen Square China has been defined as a very different place that has emerged from isolation to one of the world's significant leading players.

10 City of Politico-Religious Reasons

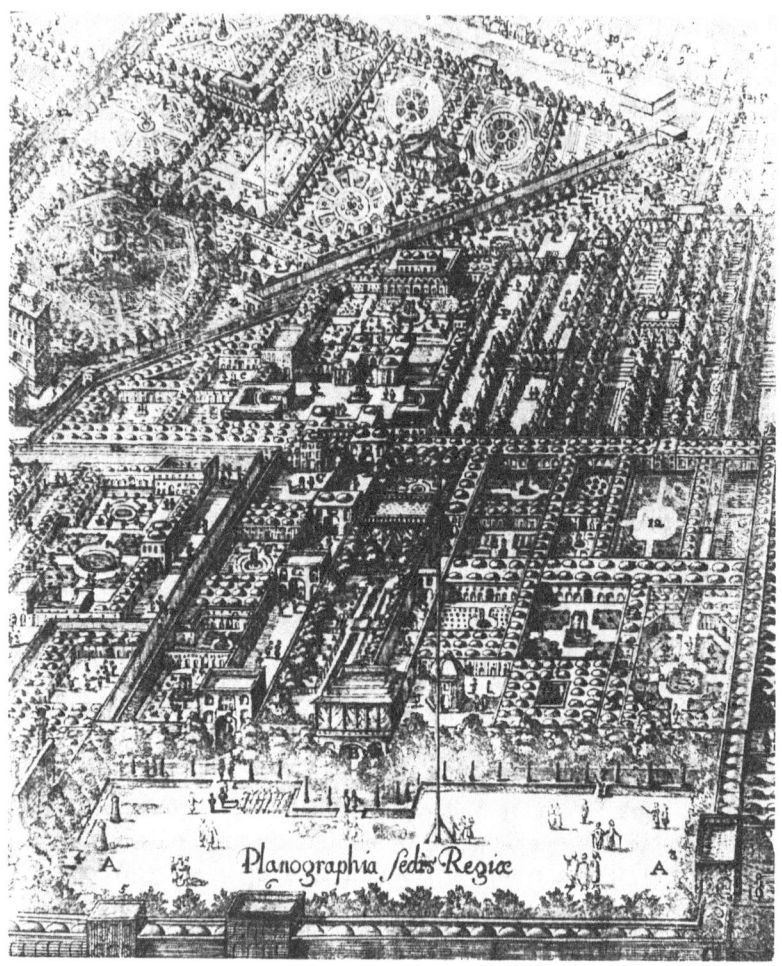

Figure 1.1 Heinz Luschey, Negelbert Kaempfer Planographia the palace district of Isfahan.

Source: Drawing 1684–1685 engraving from 1712, *British Institute of Persian Studies*, Vol. 17(1979): 75.

The historical etymology of the word equivalent in European languages brings us to Greek Agora as a political platform and Forum in Roman politics. Agora is an archetypal public space for the European city as irregular and unenclosed gathering place. The Greek Agora was represented as the essential component of a free *polis*, a symbol of democracy and the rule of law (Webb 1990, 28–29). Murray

Bookchin, political philosopher, in his book—*The Rise and Decline of Citizenship*—presents us with the evolution of various public spaces in the different ancient cities such as the earliest in Sumer centering around temples; later ones, such as Babylon in Sumer where the urban spaces were centering around templates and palaces. However, the more dynamic Greek democracies around civic squares enhance citizen conversation; medieval and more recent ones, around various marketplaces (Bookchin 1992, 5). As Murray Bookchin suggests, the city is a shapeless blob, a mere chaos of structures, streets, and squares if it lacks the institutions and forms appropriate to the development of active citizenship (Bookchin 1992, 55). Following Marshal Berman and Richard Sennett, Bookchin (1992) defined the squares and streets "as the structural essence of urbanism, particularly in the form of wide boulevards in which the monadic ego of our time can display itself in dandy like fashion and assert its' individuality" (26).

Agora is defined as the limited space in which civic engagement, teaching, religion, recreation, social and cultural engagements, participation, and direct participatory democracy could be achieved (Mehan 2017a; 2017b). Based on this definition, Agora was a political and a religious center, a place of complex associations, a place for producing craft, buying, and selling, but also a place for law, politics, philosophy, and religion (Mehan 2016b). Designed as the large triangular-shaped marketplace, the first Greek Agora was designed as the primary crossroad in Athens's city center. In contrast to the Greek Agora, Roman Forums were designed differently in each city to symbolize union, trade market, and meeting node. *Fora Civilica* and *Fora Venalia* were the center of the city's political, religious, and social life places for assembly and sale of fish (Webb 1990 29–31). The present remains of the Agora, the central market of the Roman city of Smyrna in Izmir, Turkey, date from about the second century AD. As Bookchin (1992) argues, "it could be seen daily in public squares where heated discussions over political issues intermingled with the chitchat of personal and financial problems; it assembled with almost weekly regularity on a hillside of Athens, the *Pnyx*, where meetings of the *ekklesia* were convened, or it gathered in open spaces of the Roman Forum where the *comitia tributa* often held its sessions" (52). In the Agora of Smyrna, located in Izmir, Turkey, a statue of Demeter was uncovered together with another of Poseidon (Akurgal 1973). Like Agora, "Stoa" was defined as the covered walkway or portico for public use. Stoa was surrounded by the marketplaces and sanctuaries and formed a business point and public promenade (Encyclopedia Britannica 2013).

12 City of Politico-Religious Reasons

Based on Encyclopedia Britannica's definition, the Italian piazza, square or marketplace, surrounded by buildings and approached by various streets, is associated with the French and English "place" and Spanish "plaza," all ultimately derived from the Greek plateia, "broad street." It also has the special meaning "the veranda of a house." The name became more widely used from the sixteenth to the eighteenth century, denoting any ample open space with buildings. In seventeenth- and eighteenth-century England, long covered walks or galleries with roofs supported by columns were called piazzas. In the United States during the nineteenth century, the piazza was another name for a veranda formed by projecting eaves (Encyclopedia Britannica 2020).

The term Meidan has pre-Islamic roots in mai-ta-ni (hippodrome), and in the case of Iranian cities, each had at least one major square used for business and public gatherings (Mehan 2016b; 2016c; 2016d). Originally meant horse-racing ground, this ottoman legacy from the Arabic and Persian roots is a gathering place of people to come together, play polo, horse riding, and especially to see the shows as the gathering point (Mehan 2016b). In the pre-Islamic period, during the Sassanid Empire (224–651 AD), squares were positioned near the royal palaces and gates, where bazaars opened up, so it was not shaped as a "planned" urban element and mainly served for the military services and commercial trades (Mehan 2014). The conquest of Iran by Islam (637–651 AD) led to the eventual decline of Zoroastrian religion and beliefs in Iran (Arnolds 1896). After the rise of Islam, the mosques as the religious focal points started to be added to the previous essential elements of the Sassanid cities. Therefore, the main gathering urban spaces have been the platforms of mosques and bazaars (Figure 1.2).

The Arabic-Persian dictionaries of the period from the tenth to the thirteenth centuries CE offer a rich and relatively unused source for the cultural history of that period (Durand-Guédy, Mottahedeh and Paul 2020, 465). The Arabic words for city, al-Madīna and balad (town or district), are translated as šahr in Farsi. The market (Arabic: sūq, Persian: bāzār) receives more thorough coverage than the mosque. The Arabic word for "plaza," fināʾ, is translated as "opposite the market," barābar-i sarāy. Maydān, the word for "square," is used in both Persian and Arabic, rendering siprīs or asbrīs or asprīs meaning "place for running horses" (Durand-Guédy, Mottahedeh and Paul 2020, 473).

The very notion of Ērānšahr as the new political entity introduced by Sassanid referred to the walled urban space to demarcate an actual boundary around this empire, which was considered sacred. In Ērānšahr, the governors (ostāndār), priests (mow), accountants (āmārgar), and others were involved in an unprecedented level of

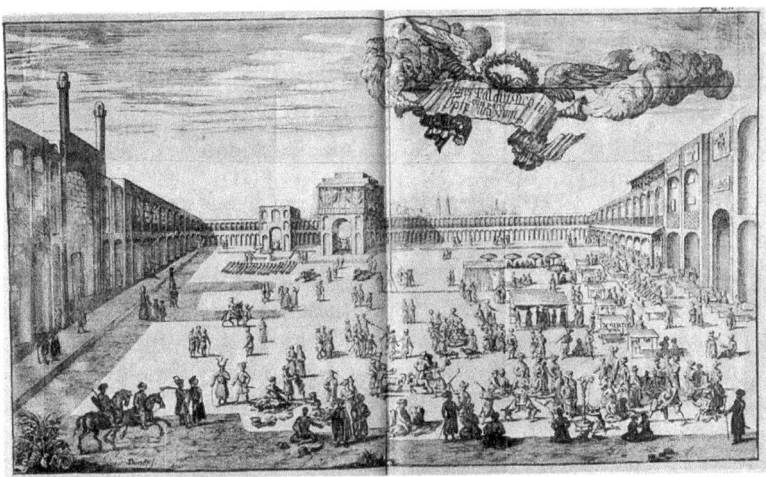

Figure 1.2 Kaempfer's drawing of the maydan of Naghsh-e Jahan (late seventeenth century). As in the illustration, not only did shops surround the maydan, but also its central space accommodated various entertainment and commercial activities.

Source: Engelbert Kaempfer, *Am Hofe des Persischen Grosskönigs: 1684–1685* (Basel, 1977).

control and centralization (Daryaee 2018). Inspiring from Greco-Mesopotamian style in the realm of art and architecture, the meaning of the square in Iran as the center of cultural, economic, and official exchanges has primarily derived from the spatial planning and urban design of the Seleucid Empire (312–364 BC) (Mohammadzadeh-mehr 2003). The city of Jūr, later known as Fīrūzābād, was a circular city, perhaps the most famous of the Sassanid cities divided by radical roads, drainage ditches, and irrigation channels, some extending to more than 5 kilometers beyond the double walls of the town. The roads divided the city into 20 sectors within the city walls (ca. 2000 m in diameter), and there are three concentric ring-roads (Durand-Guédy, Mottahedeh and Paul 2020, 80).

The formation and development of Iranian cities took shape in association with the state authority, religion, geography, and governmental headquarters. The spatial layout of, from private to public, culture to power, and shadow to light, is resembled in the city of *Persepolis* or *Parse*, which was built in 518 BC, situated 60 kilometers north east of Shiraz with no existing prototype. Persepolis holds excellent attention in architecture and city planning because of its alleys, streets, and public spaces, indicating an advanced spatial

14 *City of Politico-Religious Reasons*

planning stage. Inspired by Mesopotamian models, at Persepolis, the public quarters, including the central square, were separated from more private quarters. This interplay of transition from the introverted (andarun) and extroverted (birun) spaces with a multiplicity of interplays was the main characteristic of Iranian spatial languages and architectural archetypes (Rajendran et al 2021).

Following Eugen Wirth's arguments, describing the urban features of Iranian cities by categorizing them as the "Islamic cities" is misleading since the characterizing features of Iranian cities, apart from the central mosque, were in place before the coming of Islam. Using the term "Oriental cities" did not gain broad acceptance since the recent research has bypassed any such questions of macro-sociological classification or analysis (Wirth 2000). According to Gaube, Iranian cities were frequently planned and founded with a circular perimeter around a rectangular grid. Gaube had identified an "eastern Iranian" type of city: with a square plan, rectangular grid, one gate in each of the four walls, and a citadel, which might be part of the defensive wall or stand at some distance from the city proper (Gaube 1979).

In the lands dominated by various social and religious practices of Islam, the architectural concept of the Meidan (Or Arabic Maydan) may have taken myriad shapes, also reflecting the ontological multi-layered hybridity of the term itself. The idea of an articulated public urban space in the early cities of late Antiquity, where newly arrived or converted Muslim residents integrated into their urban planning, the functional and spatial possibilities presented by the survival and memories of the Roman Fora and Byzantine hippodromes (Babaie and Grigor 2015). *Rabbat* argues that the main congregational mosque's open space may consciously replace the Agora in both its urban and political functions. *Rabbat* states that the type of open space, called Maydan, already existed in the Arab cities. It was introduced as a hippodrome for equestrian exercises when military dynasties ruled most Arab towns in the pre-modern period (Rabbat 2012, 198–208).

Baghdad (Arabic: city of Peace), situated in the heart of Mesopotamia, was founded in 762 as the capital of the Abbasid dynasty of caliphs. Known as the "Round City," the very center was empty except for the two important buildings: The Friday Mosque and the Caliph's main headquarters for guards, a direct reflection from the Persian Sassanid Urban Design, the manifestation of the integration between temporal and spiritual sovereignty. Influenced by the Apadana design of ancient Iranian architecture and Sassanid palace design, the mosque was the premier public space in Baghdad, the equivalent of the Agora in the ancient Greek city, and the public square in the medieval European town (Grabar 2006). The tower square was at the center of the town and had a symbolic significance as the focal point of the empire. It was also essential for measuring the radial lines, which in the eighth century became the model for the plan of Baghdad (Gester 2010).

Uncovered Courtyard of the City: The Delights of Earthly Paradise

The Greek word παραδεισος [*paradeisos*] was adopted from Old Persian *paridayda* and initially borrowed by the Greek philosopher and historian Xenophon of Athens. The term consists of the two words: "*pairi*" ("around") and "*daeza*" or "*diz*" ("wall," "brick," or "shape"), and refers to the supreme bliss of Eden, "a heavenly place," a *paradise*, or the reward of the faithful those who responded to God's commands as promised in the Jewish, Christian, and Islamic texts—initially dominated by a single noun denoting an "enclosed garden/walled enclosure." The earthly image of Paradise is illustrated in Athanasius Kircher's *Arc Noë*, which displays an image of existence inside Paradise. It is depicted as an enclosed domain between the Tigris and Euphrates in Mesopotamia. It is formed as a walled square plan; four gates, guarded by four angels, face the four cardinal points. In the middle, two bodies of water meet, and the tree of life is located, where Adam and Eve are illustrated positioned in the bottom left corner of Paradise (Kircher 1675, 230).

This archetype of the enclosed paradise gardens has been associated etymologically with the historical Achaemenid precedents, interpreted as an earthly symbol of celestial Paradise. Belonged to Cyrus, Pasargadae in the province of Fars is the old intact layout. Later in the Sassanid period, the fortified walls built in the sixth century CE around *Ērānšahr* are often connected to the notion of a paradise; a walled garden, in which the city is imagined as the garden and the king would act as the gardener (Lincoln 2012, 5–19). In the *Shāhnāmeh* of Ferdowsī, King Khusrow (also known as *Anushirvan*) delivered an excellent speech about Iran as a garden and its walls:

> *Iran is like a lush spring garden*
> *Where Roses ever bloom*
> *The army and weapons are the garden's walls*
> *And lances its wall of thorns*
> *If the garden's walls are pulled down*
> *Then there would be no difference between it and the wilderness*
> *[beyond]*
> *Take care not to destroy its walls*
> *And not to dishearten or weaken Iranians*

*If you do, then raiding and pillaging will follow
And also, the battle-cries of riders and the din of war
Risk not the safety of the Iranians' wives, children, and lands
by bad policies and plans.*

(Khaleghi-Motlagh 1988–2008, 275–282)

The ideal concept of the city for the Persians was firmly bound to the ultimate goal of creation and the microcosms image of original perfection, which according to Mazdaean-Zoroastrian ideology is "happiness for mankind." The dichotomy between inside and outside of Ērānšahr, in a similar fashion as the Evil Spirit (Ahriman), causes cosmic chaos against Ohrmazd (the supreme God). These monsters (an-ēr) reside outside the walls, in the desert wilderness where there is no order or law, while the ērānagān (Iranians) stay safe within the walled garden (Daryaee 2018). According to Achaemenid inscriptions, it is the King's (the emperor's) duty to restore the lost happiness of humankind. It has been written in Darius's tomb (Naqš-i-Rostam): "The great God is Ahura Mazda; who created the earth; who created the sky; who created mankind; who established happiness for mankind; who made Darius the king..." (Lincoln 2012).

In line with Aristotle, Farabi, the early Islamic Philosopher, in his political treatises premises that the humans can only attain the perfection they are destined to inside the ideal *Madina*, as a whole, considering its governance and administration. Farabi emphasized that this condition is an archetypical form of the built environment to expand the empire, peace, and happiness. In Farabi's political philosophy, the ideal medina is a city-state that guarantees the most significant possible degree of pleasure to its citizens, based on the perfection of the human nature by which the philosopher ruler governs. According to Farabi (1993), in a democratic city-state regime, each individual is the judge of what constitutes happiness:

> The democratic city is the one in which each one of the citizens is given free rein and left alone to do whatever he likes. Its citizens are equal and their laws say that no man is in any way at all better than any other man. Its citizens are free to do whatever they like; and no one, be he one of them or an outsider, has any claim to authority unless he works to enhance their freedom. Consequently, they develop many kinds of morals, inclinations, and desires, and they take pleasure in countless things.... This city brings together the groups- both the base and the noble- that existed separately in other cities.
> (50)

According to *Lehrman*, the threefold attraction of establishing gardens in Iran is as follows: first, based on many references to the Paradise Garden in the Quran, the idea of paradise was associated as a reward for the faithful. The second was the secular tradition of the royal pleasure garden in Iran. The third was the particular response to the climate demands in Iran, with its predominant dryness and heat and lack of water availability (Lehrman 1980, 32).

Courtyard houses became a generic typology in hot, arid, climatic landscapes, and formed the basis of urban patterns in the Iranian cities (Edwards et al 2006, 15). The Courtyard provides a private, protected space, symbolizing an individual's inner life. The only elements allowed in emptiness are the vital natural elements: green and water. In practice, it supplies light and cool air to the rooms that form it. Fountain, pool, shade, and occasional trees are also symbolic reflections of the terrestrial incarnation of heaven. Moreover, the Courtyard, having been defined by the house itself and high walls, is "open to sky" space and is used primarily as an extension of the living quarters (Edwards et al 2006, 15).

Central courtyards between masses of solid volumes reflect the critical role of emptiness in Iranian architecture. The typical enclosed and central courtyards were prevalent in Mesopotamian and Iranian houses used in Iranian square on a grand scale (Mehan 2016b). For Nader Ardalan, "The courtyard as the manifestation of the centripetally oriented form of the microcosm, the hidden, may be viewed as mutually complementing and thereby completing aspects of spaces" (Ardalan and Bakhtiar 2000, 68). *Kamran Afsharnaderi* similarly conceived the Iranian plaza as a city courtyard, emphasizing its boundaries while the center is always empty (Figure 1.3). The idea of a central space, as an introverted characteristic, is implied explicitly in courtyards or urban squares that are regarded as "uncovered courtyard of the city" (Afsharnaderi 2007).

Square as Non-Choice: The Political Locus of Sovereignty

The term "sovereignty" was understood as "suzerainty" and identified only the feudal powers of lordship and patrimonial rights of monarchs in medieval European times. In this definition, the state is the institutional entity distinct and autonomous from the sovereign (the ruler) and comprises territory, people, and institutional form (Loughlin 2004, 208). This move, of course, extends since sovereignty is held to be concentrated or dispersed in the social body, or turned

18 City of Politico-Religious Reasons

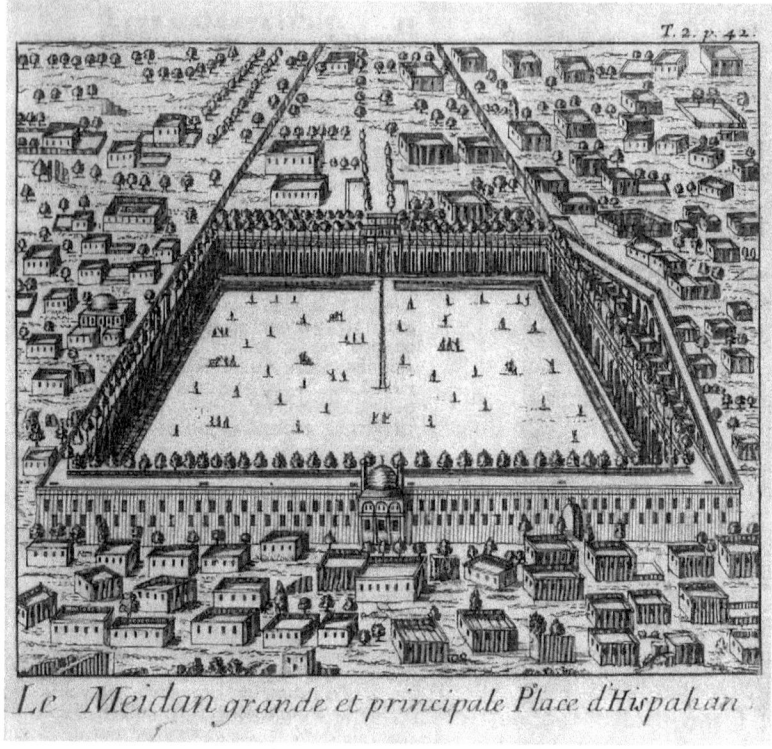

Figure 1.3 Engraving of the Maydan Naghsh-e Jahan in Tavernier. The city square is a positive void as the courtyard of the city.

Source: Bibliothèque nationale de France (gallica.bnf.fr).

into a property of the state as a whole through abstraction, the entire locus problem rests on the assumption that sovereignty is one and indivisible within the political order (Bartelson 1995, 28). Instead, the modern concept designated the relationship between the state and the people and originated with political modernization in Europe and the formation of nation-states (Loughlin 2004, 74). For *Michel Foucault*, one of the critical parts of the discipline, a technique in a disciplinary society, is control of space. The other way of increasing authorities' power is by bringing similar people in a place to absorb others who share the same belief and giving sacred values to the place. From an operational point of view, the question of the loci of sovereignty is lumped together under the organizing principle of hierarchy, with no further elaboration (Foucault 1995).

The Safavid dynasty (1501–1736 AC), which approximately coincides with European Renaissance, often referred to as the first geopolitically stable dynasty after the introduction of Islam to Iran which throws up the central issues concerning the relationship between mysticism, religion, sovereignty, power, and nation-state (Blair and Bloom 1995). Examining the Safavids from their foundations in the fourteenth century to their relations with the rest of the world in the eighteenth century shows the importance of the Safavid's sovereignty in situating Iran in a broader, regional, and global context. However, a closer examination of the layout of Isfahan shows the combined principles of Turco-Iranian urban forms and Perso-Islamic and Timurid garden patterns (Walcher 1998, 33).

One of the Safavids' most important decisions was to propagate an official state doctrine of Twelve Shi'ism, the construct of Sunni-Shi'ite polemics that continues to characterize the Middle East and the Islamic world into the twenty-first century (Mitchell 2010). As an important, influential hub for Shi'a Muslims, many Shi'a clergies immigrated to Iran from Lebanon and Bahrain during the Safavid period. The Safavid conception of a charismatic form of authority in the uniquely Perso-Shi'i imperial ideology necessitated its performance's practical architectural and urban accommodation. The spatial and visual representations of power in Safavid Iran peaked in the dramatic synergies cast across the urban spaces, the palaces, and the ceremonial practices of conviviality. The Safavid conceptualization of absolute rule couched this fundamental feature of Islam in the doctrinal framework of Twelver Shi'ism, thus laying claim to the universal authority of the Prophet while localizing this claim through the intricately intertwined features of classical Muslim and ancient Persian features of kingship (Babaie 2018, 5).

In the Safavid period, when *Shi'ism* spread throughout the country, public religious ceremonies such as rituals of *Moharram* and *Ramadan*—in which people had active roles both as spectators and performers—intensified the need for public spaces. *Tekkiyes* and *Hosseiniyes* (halls used as religious ceremonies) began to build to meet their needs (Kheirabadi 2000). According to early modern conceptualizations of the empire, absolutism, legitimacy, and authority meant that the king was above and beyond the mandate, the earthly, and the accessible. The processes of conceptualization and consolidation of this enterprise of kingship took several turns, including a less exaggerated, more normative practice integrated into the institutions of imperial authority. In this way, the Safavid imperial legitimacy rested on twin claims of descent both from the "terrestrial" lineage of Persianate kings ancient and recent and from the "celestial" origin that began with Imam Ali and continued through the family of Prophet Mohammad. The Safavid shahs' position had to be negotiated by the politico-cultural crafting, through the discharge of justice, generosity, and righteousness, of a terrestrial vision of the promised kingdom, a mirror-image, if still imperfect, of the celestial paradise made palpable here on earth. Isfahan became the embodiment of this promised paradise city (Babaie 2018, 7).

In the seventeenth century (1598–1722 AD), Isfahan projected rooted cosmopolitanism as a megacity that anchored on the conceptual and functional grandeur of the city (Babaei 2003). The strategic location of Isfahan, abundant water supply, and fertile land facilitated the development of Isfahan in the seventeenth century as Safavid's new political capital (Babaei 2003). Thomas Herbert compared Isfahan's rise as the symbol of Safavid hegemony with the grandiose supremacy of ancient royal palace cities like *Babylon* and *Persepolis* (Herbert 1928, 153).

The very demonstration of the ideological power of the Safavids manifested in the grandiose urban projects in the time of Shah Abbas, who chose the city of Isfahan as the new capital of Iran (Walcher 1998, 330). Although Lawrence Lockhart argues that Isfahan was no creation of Shah Abbas, for it has been a great city long before his reign, it had moreover been at times the capital of the country (Lockhart 1967). The old city had narrow winding streets, and the old square was oriented toward Mecca. The new master plan of Isfahan as the imperial capital of the Safavids differentiated the new urban center from the historical core by the street patterns organization on the orthogonal grids not oriented toward Mecca. Carl Ritter (1840) called it "die Paradiesische Stadt" in the early nineteenth century to celebrate Isfahan's beauty and extol its pre-eminence as an imperial city. In their most remarkable manifestations, Isfahan's master plan was inspired by both ideas of self-conscious Persian paradise and Islamic Medina. Starting from 1597 to 1598 and at the direct order of Shah Abbas, several civic and royal urban projects had already begun, which were anchored on the main public square and a boulevard.

This exquisite architectural design happened in the formation of a unique spatial configuration of Meidan, which was a rectangular space surrounded by bazaars and served as the forecourt to the royal palaces, gardens, and mosques and contributed to social and political activities. The placement of the monumental structures strategically articulated the four sides of the Meidan: the royal bazaar (Qaysariyye, begun in 1590/1591) on the north side linking the new urban center to the old through its vaulted markets; the Ali Qapu

Palace (1590/1591–1615) on the west, also serving as the ceremonial entrance into the palace; the Sheikh Lotf-Allah Chapel-Mosque on the east; and the spectacular new congregational mosque (the Royal Mosque, 1611–1638) on the south (Babaie and Grigor 2015).

By the seventeenth century, the square and its attached institutions were not only the ceremonial sites of sovereignty but also the integrated sites of commercial, civic, religious, and political interactions. In this layout, the royal compound was connected to the city through the intermediary space of Meidan; this was sustained as a precedent for Iranian cities over the next three centuries. The Meidan-e Naqsh-e Jahan, the Image of the World Square, measures about 83,000 square meters, second only to Tiananmen Square in Beijing in area, or seven times the size of Piazza di San Marco in Venice (Figure 1.4). Mao also dramatically reconfigured Tiananmen Square, turning what had long been a modest T-shaped palace into a vast masonry expanse intended to be able to assemble one million Party faithful (Vale 2008, 31). Thomas Herbert noted, "The Meidan is spacious, as pleasant and aromatic a market as any in the universe. It is a thousand paces from North to South, and from East to West above two hundred, resembling our Exchange, or the Place-Royal in Paris, but six times larger" (Herbert 1928, 127).

Figure 1.4 Meydan-e Naghsh-e Jahan in Isfahan by Eugène Flandin, 1851.
Source: Voyage en Perse, avec Eugène Flandin, éd. (Gide et Baudry, 1851).

22 City of Politico-Religious Reasons

The Chahar Bagh Avenue, a 4-kilometer long, verdant public promenade, served principally as an arterial link between the older northwestern neighborhoods of Isfahan and its new residential quarters. The word Chahar-bagh or charbagh means "four gardens," containing symbolic descriptions of paradise, which is recognized as an archetype referred to the garden of this type at Pasargadae in Iran. It refers to a famous garden typology consisting of four plots divided by waterways or paths, forming a cruciform plan. Chaharbagh is the main boulevard of Isfahan (Iran), built between 1596 and 1957 by the Safavid Shah Abbas I. The other synonyms meant to be a retreat from the desert include *Jannat* in Arabic and *Ferdows* in Farsi—meaning paradise/garden in both languages. Additionally, some Qur'anic verses suggest the existence of four paradises that is also represented by the Chahar-bagh design. The four parts of the Chahar-bagh symbolize and represent the four rivers in the celestial paradise mentioned in the Qur'anic verses, which inspires the four-part design of the Persian garden.

The new Meidan aligns with the new promenade called *the Chaharbagh* (1596–1602) and the multi-ethnic, multi-faith sacred sites in the south part of the Zayanderud River. The 1.9 kilometers boulevard (*the chaharbagh*), a Persian garden type of considerable historical significance for Islamic societies, comprises a four-quadrant sub-division of a lot, usually enclosed, was an impressive urban intervention. In Isfahan, the Chaharbagh Promenade was built as the north-south axis of the new capital to connect the new center of the city (*the* Meydân) to the royal quarters over the river. This comprehensive project is comparable to similar urban interventions in Rome by *Pope Sixtus V*, which had launched just a few years before (Tournikiotis 1955, 41). In between the two foci of Isfahan—the Meidan and Chahar Bagh—the other residential, institutional, religious, political, and economic parts of the city have been situated. Some historical, cultural, political, and geographical features of Naghsh-e Jahan Square in other Iranian squares such as Saheb-Abad and Saadat-Abad show their common ideological origins.

Major Findings

This chapter defines the city as a sovereign political community, which modernity transformed its urban form and social function. This chapter analyzed the square beyond a mere architectural element in the city but suggested the idea of Meidan as the core of the projects on the city, which historically exposed in formalization of theological ideology. It weaves this archetype with its contemporary socio-political atmosphere as a new paradigm. Therefore, here, the concern is the issue of continuity, a specific conception of space, which has remained constant through time: (re)reading the city as a series of Meidan. Building upon this theoretical framework, respectively, the historical, social, and political concept of Meidan—a term that has applied mainly for the Iranian public squares—is reintroduced in the first part. Through the case of Meidan, this chapter analyzed the relationship between religion and imperial politics both as an ideological model of empire and as a microcosmic image of original perfection. Since this chapter aims to connect the fundamental archetypes, thoughts, ideologies, foundations, and frameworks in Iranian art, architectural and urban history, the most predominant concepts of political squares from pre-modern time to present in shaping the ideogram of the city are analyzed and discussed.

References

Afsharnaderi, Kamran. 2007. *The Gardens of Paradise*. Tehran: Kelk.
Akurgal, Ekrem. 1973. *Ancient Civilizations and Ruins of Turkey-From Prehistoric Times Until the End of The Roman Empire*. Istanbul: Haşet Kitabevi.
Ardalan, Nader, and Laleh Bakhtiar. 2000. *The Sense of Unity: The Sufi Tradition in Persian Architecture*. Chicago: The Kazi Publications.
Arnolds, Thomas Walker. 1896. *The Preaching of Islam: A History of Propagation of the Muslim Faith*. Westminster: A. Constable and Company.
Babaei, Susan. 2003. "Persia: The Safavid 1501-1722." In *The Great Empires of Persia*, by Jim Masselos, 139–235. London: Thames and Hudson.
Babaie, Susan. 2018. *Isfahan and Its Palaces*. Edinburgh: Edinburgh University Press.
Babaie, Susan, and Talinn Grigor. 2015. *Persian Kinship and Architecture: Strategies of Power in Iran from the Achaemenids to the Pahlavis*. London: I. B. Tauris & Co Ltd.
Bartelson, Jens. 1995. *A Genealogy of Sovereignty*. Cambridge: Cambridge University Press.
Barthes, Roland. 1989. *Empire of Signs*. New York: Hill and Wang Press.
Blair, Sheila, and Jonathan Bloom. 1995. *The Art and Architecture of Islam: 1250–1800*. Yale: Yale University Press.
Bookchin, Murray. 1992. *Urbanization Without Cities: The Rise and Decline of Citizenship*. Montreal/New York: Black Rose Books.
Britannica, Encyclopedia. 2013. "Stoa." *Encyclopedia Britannica*, February 26.
Britannica, Encyclopædia. 2020. *Piazza*. 02 07. Accessed 11 18, 2021.
Daryaee, Touraj. 2018. *The Sasanians and the Late Antique World*. Mizan: Journal for the Study of Muslim Societies and Cavillations 3:19–39.

Durand-Guédy, D., R. Mottahedeh, and J. Paul. 2020. *Cities of Medieval Iran*. Leiden: Brill.

Edwards, Brian, Magda Silbey, Mohammad Hakmi, and Peter Land. 2006. *Courtyard Housing: Past, Present and Future*. London: Taylor and Francis Group.

Farabi. 1993. *The Political Regime, trans. Muhsin Mahdi*, by Ralph Lerner and Muhsin Madhi. Ithaca: Cornell University Press.

Foucault, Michel. 1995. *Discipline and Punish: The Birth of the Prison*. New York: Vintage Books.

Gaube, Heinz. 1979. *Iranian Cities*. New York: New York University Press.

Gester, George. 2010. *Paradise Lost; Persia from Above*. London: Phaidon.

Grabar, Oleg. 2006. "The Architecture of the Middle Eastern city from Past to Present: The Case of Mosque." In *Islamic Art and Beyond*, by I. Lapidus (Vol. III). Hampshire: Ashgate Publishing Limited.

Herbert, Thomas. 1928. *Travels in Persia 1627–1629*, by W. Foster. London: G. Routledge and Sons, Ltd.

Hidenobu, Jinnai. 1995. *Tokyo, a Spatial Anthropology*. California: University of California Press.

Kanda, Shun. 1974. "The Street and Hiroba of Japan." In *The Inner City*, by Declan Kennedy Margrit Kennedy, 85–86. Elek Books Ltd.

Khaleghi-Motlagh, Djalal. 1988–2008. *The Shahnameh = The Book of Kings*, by Djalal Khaleghi-Motlagh. Vol. 7. 8 Vols. vols. New York: Bibliotheca Persica.

Kheirabadi, Masoud. 2000. *Iranian Cities: Formation and Development*. Syracuse: Syracuse University Press.

Kircher, Athanasius. 1675. *Arca Noè*. Amsterdam: J.Janssonium a aesbege.

Lehrman, Jonas Benzion. 1980. *Earthly Paradise: Garden and Courtyard in Islam*. Los Angeles: University of California Press.

Lincoln, Bruce. 2012. *'Happiness for Mankind': Achaemenian Religion and the Imperial Project*. Leuven: Peeters.

Lockhart, Lawrence. 1967. *Shah Abbas's Isfahan*. London: Cities of Destiny.

Loughlin, Martin. 2004. *The Idea of Public Law*. Oxford: Oxford University Press.

Mehan, Asma. 2014. "Recreation Architectural Values of Sarvestan Garden and Pavilion." *Cultural Heritage. Present Challenges and Future Perspectives* (Università Roma Tre).

Mehan, Asma. 2016a. "Investigating the Role of Historical Public Squares on Promotion of citizens' Quality of Life." *Procedia Engineering* 161: 1768–1773.

Mehan, Asma. 2016b. "Blank Slate: Squares and Political Order If City." *Journal of Architecture and Urbanism* 40 (4): 311–321.

Mehan, Asma. 2016c. "Public Squares and Their Potentials for Social Interaction: A Case Study of Historical Public Squares in Tehran." *Proceeding of World Academy of Science, Engineering and Technology* 10 (2).

Mehan, Asma. 2016d. "Squares as Tools for Urban Transformation: Foundations for Designing the Iranian Public Squares." *Revista Brasileira De Planejamento e Desenvolvimento (Universidad Tecnológica Federal Paraná)* 5 (2): 246–254.

Mehan, Asma. 2017a. "An Integrated Model of Achieving Social Sustainability in Urban Context Through Theory of Affordance." *Procedia Engineering* 198: 17–25.

Mehan, Asma. 2017b. *The Empty Locus of Power: Production of Political Urbanism in Modern Tehran*. PhD Thesis, Department of Architecture and Design (DAD), Politecnico di Torino, Torino: Politecnico di Torino, 167.

Mitchell, Colin P. 2010. *New Perspectives on Safavid Iran: Empire and Society*. Abingdon: Routledge.

Mohammadzadeh-mehr, Farrokh. 2003. *Toopkhaneh Square*. Tehran: Moavenat-e Memari va Shahrsazi.

Rabbat, Nasser. 2012. "The Arab Revolution Takes Back the Public Space." *Critical Inquiry* 39 (1): 198–208.

Rajendran, Lakshmi, Fariba Molki, Sara Mahdizadeh, and Asma Mehan. 2021. "(Re) Framing Spatiality as a Socio-Cultural Paradigm: Examining the Iranian Housing Culture and Processes." *Journal of Architecture and Urbanism* 45 (1): 95–105.

Ritter, Carl. 1840. *Die Erdkunde Von Asien*. Vol. VI. Berlin: G. Reimer.

Stevenes, James, and Susan Wilson. 2015. *A Dictionary of Architecture and Landscape Architecture (3 ed.)*. Oxford: Oxford University Press.

Tournikiotis, Panayotis. 1955. *The Histography of Modern Architcture*. Cambridge and London: MIT Press.

Vale, Lawrence J. 2008. *Architecture, Power, and National Identity*. London and New York: Routledge.

Walcher, Heidi A. 1998. "Between Paradise and Political Capital: The Semiotics of Safavid Isfahan." *Middle Eastern Natural Environment* 1: 330.

Webb, Michael. 1990. *The City Square*. New York: Watson-Guptill Publications.

Wirth, Eugen. 2000. *Die Orientalische Stadt Im Islamischen Vorderasien Und Nordafrika*. Mainz: Philipp von Zabern.

2 City of Modern Reasons

This chapter explores the planning politics that transformed Tehran by the destruction of old city walls and the construction of long boulevards through comparative analysis in the region. It aims to (re)read particular histories, local complexities, and challenges of actors in the city's planning through and the identification of the urbanization paradigms and addressing the spatial manifestations of internal mediations in Tehran's modernization. It deals with the international transfer of planning ideas through the window of—Street maps (Map of 1933 and 1937 Tehran)—during the First Pahlavi (1925–1941) reign in Tehran.

Diffusion of Planning and Urbanization Paradigms

Since a viable planning theory includes the complex dynamics of socio-political life and urban form, the comparative approach in urban studies emphasizes the commonalities across different types of cities and the organizational processes that shaped them. We learned before from studying the "circulation" of planning exported from the most developed societies and the various forms of "master planning" as part of modernization programs. However, we need a more careful "contextualized" spatial language equipped with local socio-political narratives to avoid generalizing the claims in the field of "international planning transfer."

This chapter sees the transformation of Paris as a model of modernization used as the political and morphological wheel in this research, one that influenced other cities and wishes to show it affected (directly, indirectly, or inadvertently) modern planning in Tehran. In parallel, it focuses on the Street Map of Tehran to explore the morphological metamorphoses of capital and its related transformation of social forms and political relations from the late nineteenth century to the

DOI: 10.4324/9781003140795-3

middle of the twentieth century. This draft aims to critically situate the street map of Tehran in its broader political and historical setting. While there is no shortage of research portraying Tehran's urbanization and urban growth, this premise is essential for knowledge transfer. It helps us understand how planning ideas and modernization tactics were created in one situation in the West and have traveled to the East (or/and inspired) and was implemented (or/and translated) in a different location.

Considering the complex nature of "transnational planning transfer" discipline and finding the appropriate analytical concept, this article aims to ask how in Iran—as a country never colonized—the French idea of "how to plan a street" was taken up as an ideal planning form? How would Tehran's street map analysis promote the new understanding of international planning transfer beyond what we already know? For responding to these questions, this chapter employs a mixed-method evaluation of the Tehran street map based on the political-morphological and historical-comparative analysis. Here the aim is to situate the research within the historical context and support the suggested arguments with the archival and bibliometric research, using Farsi/Persian, French, and English languages, and drawing on local materials. Also, this chapter engages meaningfully with a large body of transnational planning and comparative urban theories scholarship to stimulate the focus on the problematization of the diffusion process and the study of local meditations. By (re)reading and analyzing the planning of Tehran through different actors (in terms of sociopolitical situation and spatial concepts), this chapter aims to open up the future discussions and sketch possible lines of future research, rather than to formulate definitive concrete conclusions. The final aim is to contribute to the growing body of literature in the critical revision of modern transnational planning transfer and urban history narratives in a non-colonial, middle eastern city that was (and is) always a significant interest to colonial powers.

Circuits of Planning Paradigms and Comparative Urbanism

Planning histories offer a necessary means of recognizing the intricate patterns of collusion, negotiation, and interaction involved in the travel of urban plans, diffusion of planning paradigms, and urban policies (Nasr and Volait 2003). In particular, modern urban planning ideas emerged across Europe and beyond (particularly in colonies) in various variants through the nineteenth century (Rabinow 1989).

The emerging body of transnational planning transfer literature comprises what Patsy Healey (2013) calls scholarly "ether" or "good ideas," "circulating in a particular political, policy, or professional discourse," "awash with new directions and intellectual projects" which contains divergent aims, epistemologies, and methodologies (1511). However, instead of underpinning such flows as the "positive" and "benign" contributions by linear and singular models of development pathways—known as the "modernization myth"—Healy (2011) invites us to recognize, (re)read, and (re)consider particular histories, local complexities, and challenges of (foreign, local and indigenous) actors in different contexts, as well as the damaging consequences when external ideas about planning and development are planted upon specific histories and geographies (188).

For exploring the contemporary transnational flows of planning ideas and practices, Healy offers three central concepts, including "actor-network theory (ANT)," "discourse analysis," and "circuits of knowledge" and hegemonic projects in the globalization literature. However, for critical analysis of such flows, Healy (2013) suggests that special attention is needed to the "origin stories" of such ideas, their "traveling histories," and the "translation experiences" through which exogenous planning ideas and practices became "localized" (1510). For analyzing this complex and uneven interrelationship of diffusion patterns, Ward (2003) suggests that the power relationship between the "exporter" and the "importer" of planning (or the power relationship between the "originating" and "receiving" countries) has the central role in shaping the planning diffusion experience (55). Based on the power relations and structures of diffusion between the exporter and importer countries, Ward proposed six various types of diffusion, mostly based on the degree of freedom with which agents, foreign or indigenous, apply external planning models to shape the local urban environment. Ward (2003) suggests "synthetic borrowing," "selective borrowing," "undiluted borrowing," "negotiated imposition," "contested imposition," and "authoritarian imposition" as the different typologies of diffusion of transnational planning.

Planning has arguably a more extended engagement with the "transnational transfer" and "travel" of urban ideas, policies, and techniques, especially considering the international cross-fertilization of ideas and technologies in the creation of modern urban planning during the late nineteenth and early twentieth centuries (King, 2004). Some scholars started to ask if these "transnational planning ideas" promote a specific form of "hegemonic order" when they "land" in a particular context under the "globalization" theory. Nevertheless, what about countries like Iran that never colonized and developed as an internal choice or "selective borrowing"? King identifies the importance of multiple "local agencies" and "actors" involved in diffusion places at the center of analysis without allowing the macro-theorizing like the post-colonial theory, globalization, or World-systems to dominate the interpretation. So, the focus should be on the "multilayered" and "fragmented" categories of each city rather than relying on the general groups such as Arab, Islamic, or Colonial cities (King, 1976).

To show the connections of cities, an emerging scholarly interest highlighted the multiple spatialities of placemaking, networking, and sociopolitical relationships echo the re-emerging recognition of the comparative logic of urban studies (Mehan 2019, 10). McFarlane (2011) suggests that "the comparative city" should be studied as a mode of thought that informs how urban theory is constituted (726). Similarly, Ward (2008) suggested a "relative comparative approach" to urban and planning studies that incorporates cross-cultural studies and understands cities as the primary "focal nodes of financial flows, migration, policy formation and the practice of state power" (408). Similarly, Robinson (2011) has developed a new phase of "comparative urban" research by offering various approaches to recast the methodological foundations of a comparative approach to urban studies by analysis of "topological spatialities and power relations" (2). As Jan highlighted, "the essence of comparative urbanism should be based on investigating differences and commonalities among various cities and urban processes. Moreover, comparisons must be question-driven, theory-oriented, empirically embedded, and carefully selected cases" (Nijman 2015, 183–184).

In this way, the theoretical frameworks of comparative urbanism are research design, methodology, observation, and analyses. Besides, since state power relations and the transitionary urban paradigms and urbanization processes have formed a constant critical dimension in the evolution of cities, a broad political, historical, cultural, and social perspective can outline comparative urbanism.

The Bourgeois City Paradigms

Ildefonso Cerdà, author of the 1859 plan for Barcelona's *Eixample* (Extension), and the author of *Teoria General de la urbanización* (as the modern theoretical work on urban planning), reported that *Georges-Eugène Haussmann* has offered to buy his plans and studies, which he refused (Ward 2003, 485). Much of Paris today, including the monumental and diagonal boulevards and uniform facades, can be traced to the work of Haussmann. The state-led modernization of Paris applied strategic surgical interventions that cleared up space around the essential monumental buildings, and the introduction of municipal utilities was some of Haussmann's interventions (Paccoud 2017). The new avenues were wide enough to accommodate rails, whether underground or elevated. In this way, Haussmann's urban planning provided the latest services in terms of public health (such as aqueducts, sewers, gas streets lighting, public lavatories, designing new spaces such as public parklands for entertainment and leisure) and public transport (such as instituting forms of zoning for industry, constructing a railway route to connect the center to the surrounding areas, development of *banlieue* (the land at the edge of the city)) (McQuire 2008; Scott 1998).

On the political aspects of these urban interventions, some scholars argue that these interventions moved out of the poor and working-class populations from the city center and finally remodeled the city for the bourgeoisie (Furet 1995; Hanssen 2006; McQuire 2008). This process involved both destruction of the fragmented and socially organized neighborhood of the poor and "boulvardize" the city to surpass the future protests (Chignier-Riboulon 2011).

While the new wide avenues are conductive to control (it was more difficult to erect the barricades and circulation of government troops improved), paradoxically, they help make public claims (Douglas 2007; Parkinson 2012). Similarly, Ferguson (1991) clarified that the process modernization in Paris differed from urban renewal plans elsewhere, which were implemented by the French state as a necessary transformation for a preventive war against organized labor. By using planning as an apparatus for control, the French urban changes contain the unruly forces of modernization (McQuire 2008).

Within a few decades, there was more evidence that a much more effective transnational flow of planning ideas and practices presents itself in many planning discourses of other cityscapes (Rosner 2005, Schorske 1981, Wilson 2003). Studies of some major urban centers such as Buenos Aires, Istanbul, Cairo, Tokyo, Budapest, Mexico City, and London repeatedly demonstrate this by naming Haussmann and replicating the new wide boulevards accurately in their modern modernized planning analysis (Abu-Lughod 1971, Zender 2015, 273). In Latin America, the traces of transformation of Paris staged in different cities such as Buenos Aires, Mexico City, and Santiago, which bloomed in the second half of the century. They transformed the image of the colonial city into the "bourgeois city" of Latin America (Almandoz 2015, 34–35). The emerging discourse of planning and new achievements circulated in prestigious exhibitions, such as the *Exposition Universelle de 1876* (universal exhibition held in Paris), and influenced the urbanization of Cairo, Istanbul, and indirectly, that of Tehran (Bosworth 2007). Isma'il Pasha had been deeply impressed by this exposition in Paris; upon his return, he had a Parisian-style master plan drawn up for Cairo (Abu-Lughod 1971; Bayat 2013). Compared to Cairo, Tehran began to be thoroughly redesigned much later on: the first wide streets were implemented between 1933 and 1940 (Clark 2013, 609). Although the construction of large motorways through the middle of the old urban fabric in the cities such as Aleppo (through the French architect, André Gutton's 1954 masterplan), Beirut and Fez (under the French rule) started much later in the 1950s. It is important to note that "the Parisian model had lost much of its lure and British and American planning models were gaining momentum" (Clark 2013, 609).

The sheer scale of Haussmann's undertaking ensures that it remains emblematic of the "creative destruction" that Marshall Berman (1983) posits as the ambivalent essence of modernization. In the discourse of modern urban planning, the name of Haussmann is related to grandiose and audacious development plans. Helmer (1985) declares that Hitler ordered Speer to surpass Haussmann and construct the great hall square (Grosse Platz) as the manifestation of the totalitarian regime and the capital of Nazi-dominated Europe. Speer wanted to be the Haussmann to Hitler's Napoleon: "Hitler remembered everything about the *Ringstrasse* and wanted the New Berlin to surpass both it and Haussmann's Paris. For years he had kept sketches he had made of the monumental buildings he planned to erect along a magnificent wide tree-planned avenue running through the center of Berlin. He regarded Haussmann as the greatest city planner in history but hoped to surpass him" (Wilson, 1991, 98).

Similarly, this stance situates Haussmann's enduring appeal to Le Corbusier (1964), who concluded his *La Ville Radiuse* (The Radiant City) of 1935 by declaring: "My respect and admiration for Haussmann." Haussmann's work was widely imitated throughout different countries as a model of functional planning driven by concern for hygiene, traffic, and zoning. However, Haussmann's critics criticized the construction of wide monotonous boulevards and the destruction of historical fabric and monuments (Lamparkos 2014).

The Making of Modern Capital

Throughout the nineteenth century and beyond, the dominant challenge of urbanization that infused the planning field was building the Western "modern utopia" as it framed within industrialization and growing urban populations (Rahdari, Mehan and Malekpourasl 2019).

The last years of Haussmann's modernization of Paris (1853–1870) were concurrent with the first years of expansion and re-planning of Tehran's bastion that commissioned to *General Alexander Buhler*—the French military Engineer and instructor at *Dar ul-Funun* (established in 1851 as the first modern institution and French-language school in Iran). Buhler prepared the bastion as a clear formal copy of Vauban's system—the French military Engineer—without delivering its military function (Figure 2.1). Construction of the Tehran citadel (in the form of a polygonal plan with triangular extensions) was instead for controlling arrivals and departures and providing measures against flood (Fisher et al 1991) (Figure 2.2.). However, due to the specific topographical approaches of the land and some influential aristocrats'

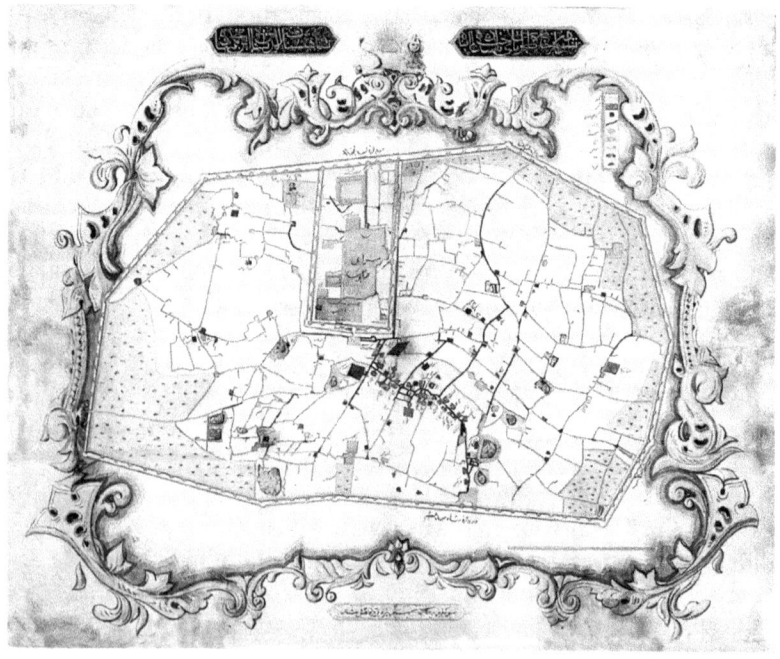

Figure 2.1 Tehran Map (Persian Version), 1852 by Russian Il'ya Nikolaevich Berezin (1818–1896), which is depicted during the reign of Nasser al-Din Shah Qajar (r. 1848–1896).

Source: Reza Shirazian. *The Guidance for Historical Maps of Tehran* (Tehran: Dastan, 2012), 11.

City of Modern Reasons 33

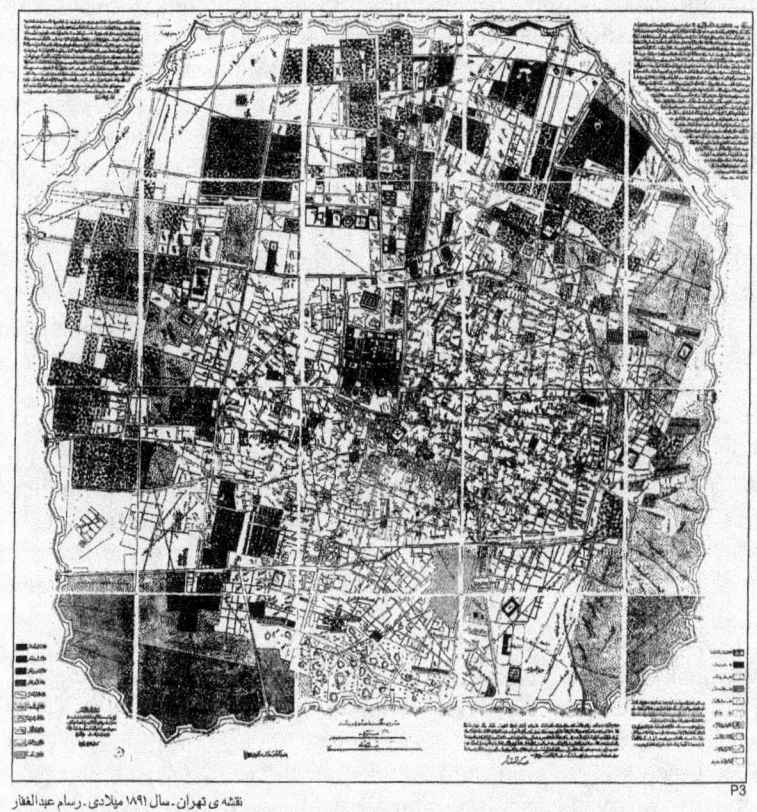

Figure 2.2 Tehran Map 1891 by Abdol-Ghaffar Khan Najmol Molk.
Source: Reza Shirazian. *The Guidance for Historical Maps of Tehran* (Tehran: Dastan, 2012), 43.

properties, the straight and broad streets were never built in 1867 urban expansion (Shirazian 2013).

Established on the site of an ancient settlement founded around 6000 BC, Tehran was part of the Median empire from around 600 BC. It replaced Isfahan as capital of Persia in 1788 AD. In the 1920s, old Tehran was demolished and re-established as the administrative, commercial, and cultural center of Iran (Morris 2016). The new morphological transformations gradually started to change the city. According to Curzon (1966), this was observable as soon as one enters the town: "We are in a city which was born and nurtured in the East, but is beginning to clothe itself at a West-End tailors. European

Teheran has certainly become or is becoming" (306). John Gurney (1992) interestingly described the city's social fabric at this time: "The city's traditional social fabric was defined by the *Mahalleh* (quarter system), which organized urban space not along class lines but according to ethnoreligious divisions, clustering citizens of the same ethnic or religious affiliation, whether rich or poor, within particular quarters" (51–71). The quarter system is defined based on clustering the citizens of the same ethnic background or religious affiliation and tradition rather than social class segregation (which emerged shortly after the urban developments).

The city's traditional morphological pattern remained unchanged until the first half of the nineteenth century, when the vision of a "modern city" transformed Tehran into an urbanized city. The straight lines inherited from nineteenth-century urbanism were a great canvas to provide an open city with a centralized political system and administrative bureaucracy for building a modern city. Kostof (1991) represented Haussmann's planning strategies as the model of urban surgery for cities anxious to meet the needs of modern traffic (266). According to Bayat (2013), "the transformations were also partly inspired by a version of a 'modern city' derived from Baron Haussmann, whose ideas spread as the time from Paris to the Middle East and were adopted by *Khedive Isma'il* (or *Isma'il Pasha*) in Cairo and Ottoman rulers in Istanbul. However, expansion did little to alter the underlying *Mahalleh* (quarter or neighborhood) system. Social inequality within the various quarters persisted and was reinforced by a speculative land market in the early twentieth century" (154–158). For clarifying the political apparatus of planning, Milani (2004) interprets the essence of a famous square in Tehran, which was built as the first touches of modernity in the nineteenth century, as an essence of the use of urban design to prevent social uprisings and to fight against: "There was Toopkhaneh, a square whose military function and ominous name (Cannon House), was reminiscent of what Benjamin calls the 'Haussmannization of Paris': an attempt to use urban design to fight 'the barricades' and to make the city and the citadel more defensible against a popular uprising" (85).

The "Urbanization Myth" in Iran

Along with the morphological analysis of the city of Tehran, some key determinants are underlying urban interventions in this period, namely, the discovery of oil which forged the "petrolic despotism" in Iran and the British presence in southern Iran (Katouzian 1983;

Mehan and Razak 2022; Mehan 2022), the ever-shifting state-society relationship, and the influence of imperial and colonial world powers on Iran (Mehan and Behzadfar 2018). Although Iran was never a colony, it was always of significant interest to colonial and imperial forces, which, in turn, manipulated Iran's political affairs through the "indirect rule" (Mamdani 1996). The country's debts to foreign banks that resulted from expensive trips to Europe, and the exploitation of the country's resources by Russia and Britain, created an atmosphere of uncertainty and dissatisfaction among different groups that led to the Constitutional Revolution (1906–1911) that signified Iran's point of entry to the realm of modernity (Abrahamian 1982). The project of modernizing Tehran was, in fact, more minor an issue for spatial planning—which was not even a topic in Iran until the mid-1950s—than it was a concern of national "development" and "preservation" goals of a centralizing state and, hence, highly political (Mehan and Bodino 2018). It was not until the reign of Reza Shah that systematic excavations by western archeologists were able to take place at sites such as Persepolis (Figure 2.3).

Figure 2.3 Oriental Institute founder James Henry Breasted and archaeologist Ernst Herzfeld at Persepolis.

Source: Oriental Institute of the University of Chicago, Abbas Alizadeh, 2014, The Challenges of Rebuilding an Archaeological Program in Post-Revolutionary Iran. http://asorblog.org/2014/06/09/the-challenges-of-rebuilding-an-archaeological-program-in-post-revolutionary-iran/

Qajar monarchs were fascinated with "catching-up" narratives of western progress and European development. Yet, Pahlavis were interested in "trickle-down" ideas of wealth generation/distribution precisely because of oil revenues as a new financial source critical to the nascent nation-state, rendering it independent from the society, bazaar, and religious authorities. It was not Reza Shah's ambitious infrastructure and urban projects that met resistance (they were celebrated by people, religious leaders, and bazaaris) (Atabaki and Zurcher 2004; Faghfoory 1987). Instead, it was social policies of the state, some of which had started before Reza Shah's reign, which met with resistance with these groups—manifest, to name a few, in the bread riot in Tehran or water shortage in *Chaleh Meydan*, the most impoverished neighborhood in the city (Abrahamian 1969; Cronin 2005; McFarland 1985). In this way, streets, especially in Tehran became and remained to be the site of resistance during and particularly after Reza Khan's reign—as opposed to the holy shrines and royal palaces during the Qajar dynasty (for instance in the Tobacco Protest of 1981 and the 1905 Constitutional revolution). However, this was more because of what Asef Bayat (1997) has shown in his book, Street Politics: the growing marginalization (political and economic) of social groups living at the outskirt of the city who used the streets as a sort of encroachment of crucial urban spaces (Figure 2.4).

It is important to note that it was not Tehran that, in fact, first became a subject of mass urban intervention and renovation in Iran; rather, it was port oil cities like Abadan that following the discovery of oil, the establishment of the refinery, and the imperial confiscation of the oil industry and even the urban setting underwent major transformations (Bazazzadeh et al 2021) (Figure 2.5). As the result, the British colonial city building modes prevailed in the Middle Eastern region (Hauser, Zhu and Mehan 2021). In contrast to many neighboring countries in the Middle East, which were protectorates of France or England, Iran and Turkey were the only exceptions where modernization was a choice and not imposed by the colonial countries (Isenstadt and Rizwi 2008). Republican Turkey provided the closest model for the modern Iranian state formed under Reza Shah during the 1920s and 1930s (Hobsbawn and Ranger 1992). Reza Shah refused to see any country after his travel to Turkey in 1934. Wilber (1975) quotes him as saying to one of his ministers reporting on his trip to Europe, "Do not say anything more about Europe, we are going to make here and make it like Europe" (233). As Matin-Asgari (2012) suggests, Lenin, Ataturk, and Mussolini were modern heroes who had accomplished similar goals:

Figure 2.4 On Teheran's Streets, two peasants dangle their feet in the muddy waters of a jube (open sewer) and study two Western-clad Bulvardiares who are passing by.

national independence, a strengthened military, a modernized state, forced capital accumulation, and rapid industrialization.

Following his trip to Turkey in 1934 and becoming aware of Turkey's First Five-year Plan, Reza Shah borrowed the idea of "national economic development" from the Soviet Union and established the High Economic Council in 1937. That concerned Britain and the United States as a sign of a "Bolshevik plot," especially as labor-force protests erupted (Bayat 2007). The end of the First World War, following which Russia pulled out its military forces from Iran, rendered Iran a primary "Third World" concern to the West—then called the "First World." Reza Shah tried to take advantage of this power rivalry by

Figure 2.5 Tehran 1947.
Source: Llewelyn-Davies International, Shahestan Pahlavi (1976), Book I, 6.

turning back and forth to the East and West so that he could muster (financial) resources required for his (brutal) mode of modernization. This attempt was punished by Western powers, who forced him to abdicate the throne to his son and live in exile.

Street-Widening Act

The destruction of walls and gateways between 1932 and 1937 gave way to a new network of open spaces. At the beginning of the 1930s, the demographic pressure, the arrival of new motor vehicles, the trans-Iranian railway project, and the provision of the main routes for urban infrastructure (such as electricity, water, urban sewage system) led to a substantial radical transformation of Tehran (Bazazzadeh, Ghomeshi and Mehan 2022).

The idea of new widening streets and alleys of Tehran began to facilitate the movement of goods, troops, and vehicles. From 1924, the process of widening and constructing Tehran streets started with the municipality's announcement. An official public statement of notice by Tehran's *Baladieh* (municipality) has translated from Farsi to English: "Buildings that used to be in the streets and alleys of the town destroyed because they were not built based on the principles of architecture and construction engineering. Property owners have to inform municipality whenever they want to build a new building and the appointed official engineer at the construction site should supervise the whole process" (Kiani 2000, 427). In 1927, Tehran's Municipality Magazine (*Majaley-e Baladieh*) published a detailed report on the first street-widening project. This report clarified how, after successfully implementing the "Street-widening Act," "the bad looking tiny shops running along the street have been replaced by great retail stores."[1]

In 1933, the Iranian parliament approved the new "street-widening act of 1933" to construct and develop the streets and passages. This act is the first fundamental legal basis of modern urbanization in Iran. "Street-Widening Act of 1933" aimed for a new urban order in the capital and improved the quality of the built environment, making them accessible to motor vehicles. For the construction of major wide avenues, the path of old walls and gateways were torn apart and provided routes for the new boulevards and streets (Madanipour 2006). Grid street patterns, uniform facades, separation of urban functions according to inflexible zoning, wide boulevards, tree-lined sidewalks, axial spatial urban form, and symmetrical squares were the significant concepts of the "Street-Widening Act of 1933," which is also known as "street layout plan" drawn by French engineer *François De Romeiser* (Koyagi 2015) (Figure 2.6).

40 *City of Modern Reasons*

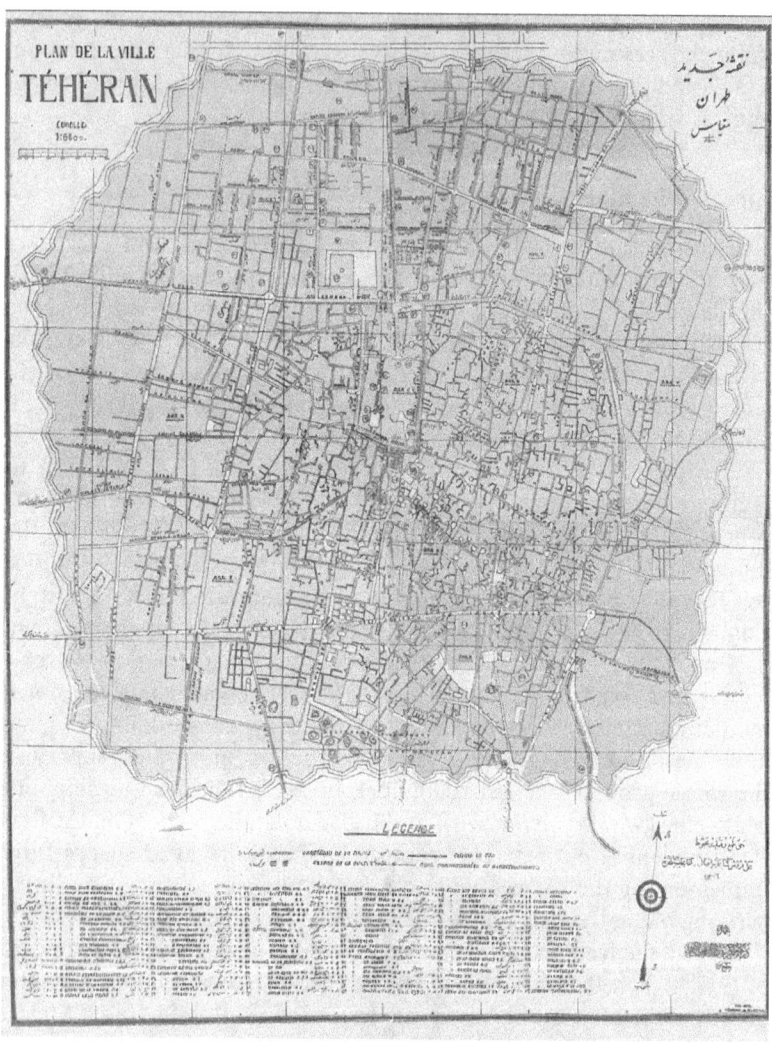

Figure 2.6 The New Map of Tehran in 1933, known as the Street Layout Plan drawn by French Engineer Francois De Romeiser. Black dotted lines show new streets within urban fabric. Red dotted lines show widening of existing streets.

Source: Reza Shirazian, *The Guidance for Historical Maps of Tehran* (Tehran: Dastan, 2012).

Alongside the construction axis of three streets including *Buzarjomehri* (currently *15-khordad* street), *Cyrus* (currently *Mostafa Khomeini*), and *Khayyam*, the expansion of some other streets such as *Rey, Molavi, Naser Khosrow, Sepah, Shahpour* (currently *Vahdat-e Eslami*), *Alaodoleh* (currently *Ferdowsi*), *Saadi*, and other small streets can be recognized in the street map of 1933. For further consideration, the detailed list of newly built streets in 1930 is attached in Table 2.1, categorized based on street names, the width of the old streets (in meter), and the new ones after extensions. In Table 2.2, you can see the amount of land (in square meters) as the result of the construction of new streets and thoroughfares (from 1927 to 1930).

Starting from 1883 to 1998 (for 115 years), Tehran had 53 mayors. Among them, *Buzarjomehri* had the longest time of the presidency (11 years) during the first Pahlavi era. Each of Tehran's mayors was the

Table 2.1 List of streets that were newly built in 1930. The table is translated into English by the author from the original archival document in Persian.

Street Names	Street Width (Before/Meters)	Street Width (New/Meters)
Sarcheshmeh St.	–	30 m
Sepah St.	23.5 m	26 m
Naderi St.	17 m	30 m
Amir Monazam St.	9.30 m	30 m
North and South St.	Near Dolab Gate	15 m
North and South St.	In front of French Embassy	15 m
North and South St.	Near Doshan Tappeh Gate	40 m
Yusef Abad St.	18 m	29 m
Jalilabad St.	12 m	30 m
Jalilabad St.	From Galobandak to Mohammadieh Square	30 m
Farhang St.	New Built	11 m
Shemiran St.	7 m	30 m
Safarabad St.	Ghasr to Darband	10 m
Dezashib St.	–	30 m
New St.	Shoa'Al Saltaneh till Sheibani Alley	15 m
New St.	Vazir Castle	10 m
By-lane	–	6 m
The New North St.	–	10 m
Nezamieh St.	17 m	30 m
Baharestan Square	55 m	30 m
Bar Square (near Bagh-e Ferdous/Ferdous Garden)	New Built	99.5 m

Source: Kiani (2000, 440).

Table 2.2 The amount of land as the result of the construction of new streets and thoroughfares starting from 1927 to 1930. The table in translated into English by the author from the original archival document in Persian.

Street Names	Year	Area (M²)
Cheragh Bargh St. (currently Amir Kabir)	1927	28240
Machine St.	1928	31923
Bazzaz St. (currently Molavi)	1928	11465
Abolfath St. (currently Molavi)	1928–1929	11298
Gomrok St. (currently Raazi)	1929	4880
Mohammadieh Square	1929	12014
Ghavam Aldoleh St.	1928	8175
Bagh Ferdows Square	1930	580
Shahpour (Farmanfarma) St. (currently Vahdat-e Eslami)	1929	21192
Takht-e Pol Alley to Nasser Al-din Alley	1929	4157
Yusef Abad (currently Jamal Al-din Asad Abadi)	1930	5817
Jannat Golshan St.	1929	4456
Moaz Al-Soltan	1929	7277
Pahlavi St to Garaheli	1929	13273
Amirieh St	1929	1064
Hasan Abad Square	1929	2519
Farhang St.	1930	571
Zaffar Aldoleh St.	1929	1435
Mahdikhani St. (currently Forozesh)	1929	6799
Naderi St. (currently Jomhori-e Eslami)	1930	13138
Shah Abad St. (currently Jomhori-e Eslami)	1929	10919
Istanbul St.	1928	4784
Sarcheshmeh St.	1928–1929	45512
Baharestan Square	1930	4452
Nezamieh St. (currently Mostafa Khomeini)	1930	3989
Sepah St. (currently Imam Khomeini)	1930	7620
Jalil Abad St. (currently Khayyam)	1930	30736
Projections in various streets	–	2254
Total	–	295550
Shemiran Road	1928	43962
Under the bridge to Tajrish Square	1930	5667
Tajrish lands that have been part of the Pahlavi Road	1929	23454
The rest of Shemiran Road to Romi Bridge (currently Shariaty)		13008
Total		86092

Source: Kiani (2000, 439).

most controversial character in the history of the Iranian municipality. During this time, General *Karim Agha Khan Buzarjomehri,* (1886–1951)—a leading Iranian military general and one of Reza Shah's most trusted figures—was appointed as Mayor of Tehran who introduced a utopian Tehran by automobiles, wide streets, electrical wagons, plumbing water, and urban sewage network (Safamanesh and Monadizadeh 1999).

The daily process of the street-widening act enforced by military agents is described as follows (the author translated the text from Farsi): "Every day the red flags are installed, and the mayor agents who are military officers arrive to demolish the houses" (Takmilhomayoun 2000). In some cases, the mayor agents arrived to demolish houses even before the house owners had enough time to move their furniture. As a result of these rapid demolitions ordered by the mayor of Tehran, people complained and asked the official parliament representatives and the local authorities to mediate and solve the problem. As a result, the statement declared by the parliament representative—*Firozie*—on February 1929 (the author translated the text from Farsi): "entering the automobiles necessitated the streets' developments, and I do not think that anyone disagrees with this, but it is better to notify the house owners and storekeepers in due time. Also, officials should compensate this damage by paying them equally compared to the house values" (Makki 1982, 452).

Regarding the financial aspect of urban interventions, *Katouzian* (1981) declared: "A clear example of bureaucratic reform and destructive maniac, was the budget spent on the renovation and beautification of the capital and other major cities, such as: making streets wider, asphalt, paved roads, enforcement of traffic regulations. However, these reforms were done superficial, irregular, erratic, and destructive. The walls and gates of the old city of Tehran as shameful symbols of backwardness demolished. In the construction of new roads or the development and widening of old streets, they demolished all the buildings in the way to direct the streets" (155). Similarly, *Shahri* argues that these urban interventions successfully solved the unemployment during this time since almost all the economic wheels put into motion, including those directly involved in construction and development part as well as the ones involved in the buying and selling of construction materials; all were busy (Shahri 1993).

It is essential to emphasize the French-influenced culture of education and Franco-Iranian relationships at this time. *André Godard, Maxime Siroux,* and *Roland Marcel Dubrulle* are the familiar French names in different sectors of Iranian cultural, artistic, architectural, and archeological societies. In addition, France was the primary destination for the new generation of Western and European-educated Iranians. Many of them sought employment with the state's national urban projects with the title of *Urbaniste-Ingenieur des Travaux Publics* (Public Works Engineer). They contributed to the new middle class's growth in this period. In 1936, the first established architectural training program was initiated by the people who graduated from France's engineering and architectural schools.

In 1937, a new plan prepared to expand the city based on the map of 1933, which put all proposals for the new boulevards circular traffic squares and widening of old streets into one master plan (Figures 2.7 and 2.8). It included a series of detailed recommendations for street adjustments, dimensions, and corners for more comfortable car circulation. In this plan, streets have drawn as open-ended interventions, and gates were replaced by traffic squares to imply physical motifs of connection and expansion (Madanipour 1998). The separation of urban functions, construction of new institutions, and flexible industrial zoning lead to a shift in the city center northward. This process resulted in the spatial segregation and polarization of the city into a prosperous and cosmopolitan north (wealth and power concentrated) and an impoverished and traditional south (new railway and industries hub) that leads to the ever-present dual-city phenomenon.

Major Findings

In "planning theory," we are continually producing, critiquing, applying, and circulating concepts, techniques, and practice experiences from one place and time to another. Much could we learn from a nuanced analysis of how planning ideas travel globally and meet various socio-historical and political-economy contexts? For example, how, why, and under conditions, specific ideas succeed, fail, are modified, embraced, or resisted. Following Patsy Healy's (2011) suggestions, this research tries to build narratives around "particular" diffusion of planning ideas to help critical learning for complex urbanized societies.

The French planning model pioneered in its ambition to treat the city as a unified space. Like Haussmann's model of urban surgery, Reza Shah's state-led urban interventions faced "formidable opposition" from property owners, clerics, and public representatives. The early phase was even reflected in the "Iranian Senate" (*Majlis*). This process radically transformed the socio-political structure of the old Tehran and gradually led to the move of the poor and working-class

City of Modern Reasons 45

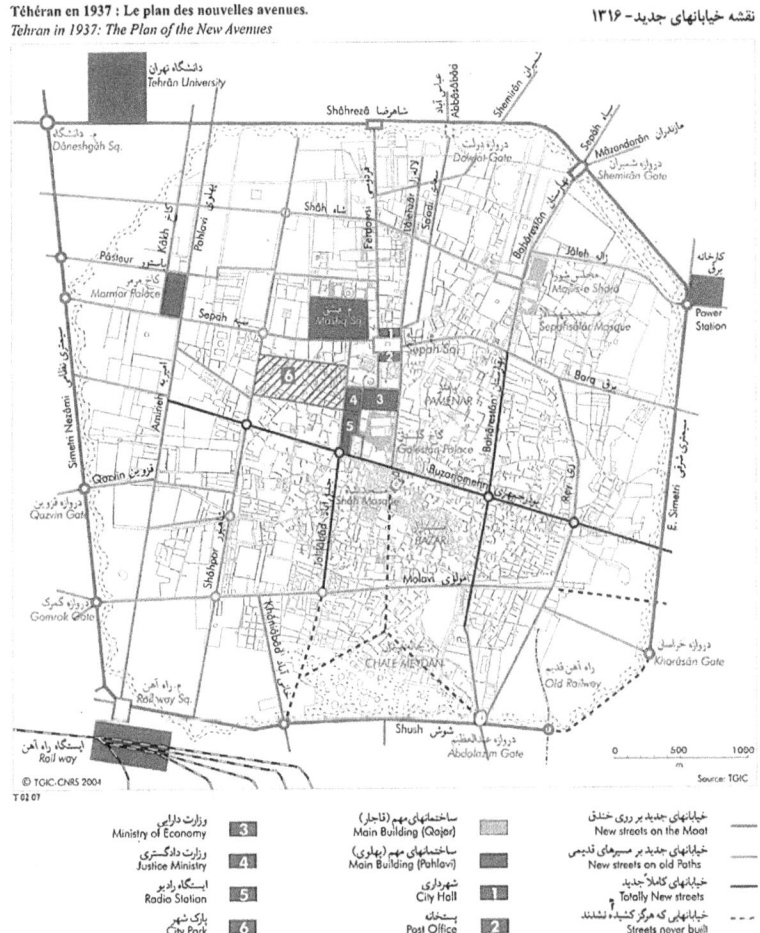

Figure 2.7 The plan of new avenues of Tehran in 1937, presents plan of the new grid of streets and emergence of new administrative buildings, in the place of old Arg, close to Bazaar.

Source: Mohsen Habibi, and Bernard Hourcade. *Atlas of Tehran Metropolis: Land & People* (Tehran: Urban Planning & Processing Company, Tehran GIS Centre, Tehran Municipality, 2005): 72.

populations from the new bureaucratic center of the city, making the north more comfortable for the emerging "bourgeoisie." One of the most intriguing aspects of this research (which is comparable with the French model) is the involvement of the military in the

46 *City of Modern Reasons*

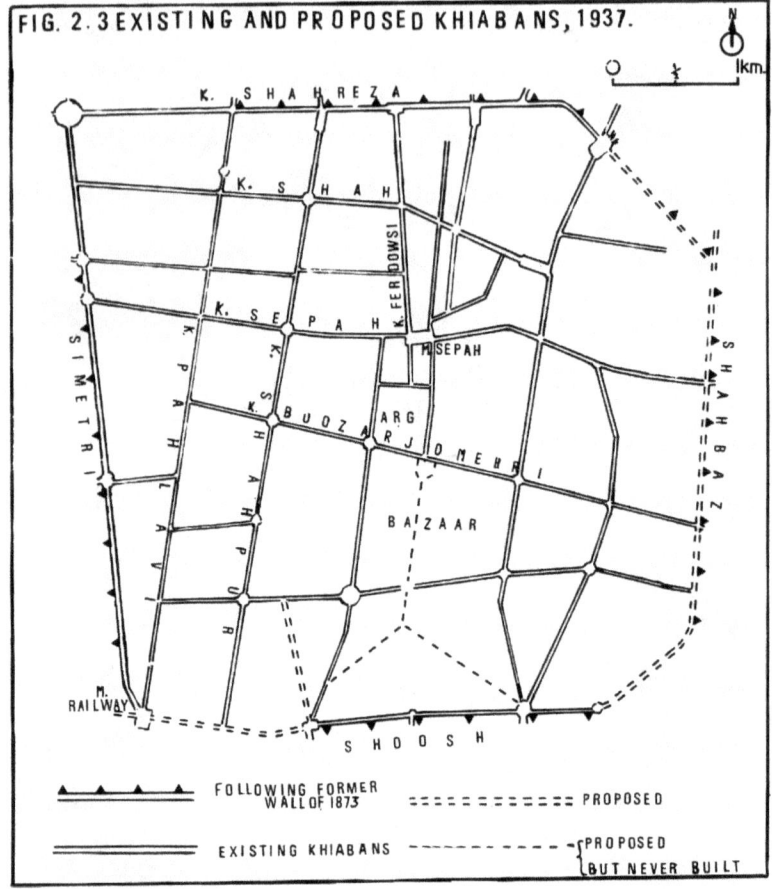

Figure 2.8 The map of existing and proposed streets, 1937.

Source: H. Bahrambeygui, *Tehran: An Urban Analysis,* Master Thesis, Durham University, Durham E-Theses, 1972: 29–30.

implementation of the plans to strengthen the control and supervision by authorities (at this time, the king and the mayor of Tehran both have the military background). It is also important to consider how planning intersects with spatial segregation patterns based on ethnic and religious criteria. Traditionally, the poor and rich cohabited in the same *Mahalleh*. In this period, the former distinctions based on religious, ethnicity, tribal, and even urban-rural divisions were substituted by the new idea of clustering the neighborhoods (and the new definition of the citizenry). Also, the "modern educational system" was modeled on the French one helped to diffusion ideas and practices. Although the adaptation of European bourgeois cultural patterns began at the elite level, the rise of the new middle class (people with a bourgeois lifestyle) started in the 1920s, concurrent with the significant urban interventions (Chehabi 2019). So, like the French model, Tehran acquired the public spaces characteristic of a "bourgeois city."

Here, the idea of "planning transfer" is accumulated around managing co-existence in a complex society like Iran by focusing on the "local" mediations, which avoids the trap of "macro-theorization" (Nasr and Volait 2003). We can consider the "transnational planning theory" field as an "evolving" and "exploratory" process that needs to "capture" the "local history" to reflect some transcendent "truth."

As Lieto (2015) suggests, instead of the primary interpretive scheme of "contextualization," "recontextualization," and "decontextualization" of planning ideas, we should instead "envisage the origin narrative of a planning idea as a mythological narrative that planners may use to refresh their knowledge and traditions each and every time an idea is put into play" (115). Here, the French planning model has been considered more than simplified empty rhetoric by putting it in the (de)contextualized inter-dialogue with localized content and socio-political relevance. The lesson that we can learn here is that the planning technique could not just be extracted from the context of the invention, "uprooted" and "planted" somewhere else. But instead, it arose from a particular ground and context and might be transplanted somewhere else with a different translation. So rather than proving the "origins" of narrative, here it is essential to learn from its relevance to other situations and different contexts.

Finally, it is essential to highlight that the city planners deal with the space intertwined with interests and powers behind any assignment. In planning theory, Friedmann (2003) argues that the discourse of planning has been shifted away from planning as an "instrument of control" to one of "innovation and action." In this way, we can define planning as a means to construct the future. However, we must build this narrative based on a practice of social, political, and historical explanation to understand how transformation happens (Unger 1998), and this article intended to take a few initial steps into that territory.

Note

1 "Khiyaban-i Cheragh Bargh," in Majaleye Baladie, issue 4, 1927 [1306]: 21–24, Archives of the library of the University of Tehran.

References

Abrahamian, Ervand. 1969. "The Crowd in the Persian Revolution." *Iranian Studies* 2 (4): 128–150.

—. 1982. *Iran between Two Revolutions*. Princeton, NJ: Princeton University Press.

Abu-Lughod, Janet. 1971. *Cairo: 1001 Years of the City Victorious*. New York: Princeton University Press.

Almandoz, Arturo. 2015. *Modernization, Urbanization and Development in Latin America, 1900s-2000s*. London: Routledge.

Atabaki, Touraj, and Erik-Jan Zurcher. 2004. *Men of Order: Authoriterian Modernization Under Ataturk and Reza Shah*. New York: IB Tauris.

Bayat, Asef. 1997. *Street Politics: Poor people's Movement in Iran*. Columbia: Columbia University Press.

Bayat, Asef. (Ed.). 2013. "Battlefield Tehran." In *Life as Politics: How Ordinary People Change the Middle East*, 153–175. Stanford: Stanford University Press.

Bayat, Kaveh. 2007. "With or Without Workers in Reza Shah's Iran: Abadan." In *The State and the Subaltern: Modernization, Society, and the State in Turkey and Iran*, by Touraj Atabaki. New York: IB Tauris.

Bazazzadeh, Hassan, Adam Nadolny, Asma Mehan, and Seyede Sara Hashemi Safaei. 2021. "The Importance of Flexibility in Adaptive Reuse of Industrial Heritage: Learning from Iranian Cases." *International Journal of Conservation Science* 12 (1): 113–128.

Bazazzadeh, Hassan, Mohsen Ghomeshi, and Asma Mehan. 2022. "The Trans-Iranian Railway: A UNESCO World Heritage Site." *TICCIH Bulletin (TICCIH)* 95: 31–33.

Berman, Marshall. 1983. *All That Is Solid Melts into Air: the Experience of Modernity*. New York: Verso.

Bosworth, Edmund. 2007. *Historic Cities of the Islamic World*. Leiden: Brill.

Chehabi, H. E. 2019. "The Rise of the Middle Class in Iran before the Second World War." In *The Global Bourgeoisie: The Rise of the Middle Classes in the Age of Empire*, by Christof Dejung, David Motadel and Jürgen Osterhammel, 43–63. Princeton and Oxford: Princeton University Press.

Chignier-Riboulon, Frank. 2011. "A Review of "Fictions of the City: Culture and Mass Housing in London and Paris." *International Journal of Housing Policy* 11 (1): 110–112.

Clark, Peter. 2013. *The Oxford Handbook of Cities in World History*. Oxford: OUP Oxford.

Corbusier, Le. 1964. *La ville Radieuse*. Paris: Quirky Books.

Cronin, Stephanie. 2005. "Popular Protest, Disorder, and Riot in Iran: The Tehran Crowd and the Rise of Riza Khan, 1921-1925." *International Review of Social History* 167–201.

Curzon, George. 1966. *Persia and Persian Question (Vol.1)*. New York: Barnes and Noble.

Douglas, Carl. 2007. "Barricades and Boulevards: Material Transformation of Paris, 1795–1871." *Interstices* 8: 31–42.
Faghfoory, Mohammd H. 1987. "The Ulama–State Relations in Iran: 1921–1941." *International Journal of Middle East Studies* 19 (4): 413–432.
Ferguson, Priscilla Parkhurst. 1991. *Paris as Revolution: Writing the Nineteenth-Century City*. California: University of California Press.
Fisher, W.B., C. Avery, C. Hambly, and C. Melvill. 1991. *The Cambridge History of Iran*. Cambridge: Cambridge University Press.
Friedmann, John. 2003. "Why Do Planing Theory?" *Planning Theory* 2 (1): 7–10.
Furet, Francois. 1995. *Revelutionary France 1770-1880*. Malden: Blackwell Publishing.
Gurney, John. 1992. "The Transformation of Tehran in the Later 19th Century." In *Teheran: Capitale Bientenaire*, by Chahryar Adle and Bernard Hourcade. Paris: French Research Institute in Iran.
Hanssen, Beatrice. 2006. *Walter Benjamin and the Arcades Project*. London; New York: Continuum.
Hauser, Stephan, Penglin Zhu, and Asma Mehan. 2021. "160 Years of Borders Evolution in Dunkirk: Petroleum, Permeability, and Porosity." *Urban Planning (Cogitatio)* 6 (3): 58–68.
Healy, Patsy. 2011. "The Universal and the Contingent: Some Reflections on the Transnational Flow of Planning Ideas and Practices." *Journal of Planning Theory* 11 (2): 188–207.
—. 2013. "Circuits of Knowledge and Techniques: The Transnational Flow of Planning Ideas and Practices." *International Journal of Urban and Regional Research* 37 (5): 1510–1526.
Helmer, Stephen D. 1985. *Hitler's Berlin: the Speer Plans for Reshaping the Central City*. First Edition. Brussels: UMI Research Press.
Hobsbawn, Eric, and Terrence Ranger. 1992. *The Invention of Tradition*. New York: Cambridge University Press.
Isenstadt, Sandy, and Kishwar Rizwi. 2008. *Modernism and Middle East: Architecture and Politics in the Twentieth Century*. Seattle and London: University of Washington Press.
Katouzian, Homa. 1981. *The Political Economy of Modern Iran: Despotism and pseudo-Modernism 1926-1979*. New York: New York University Press.
—. 1983. "The Aridisolatic Society: A Model of Long-Term Social and Economic Development in Iran." *International Journal of Middle East Studies* 15: 259–281.
Kiani, Mostafa. 2000. *Memari Dore-ie Pahlavi Avval (In Farsi)*. Tehran: Ketab-o Farhang.
King, Anthony D. 1976. *Colonial Urban Development: Culture, Social Power, and Environment*. London: Routledge & Paul.
—. 2004. *Spaces of Global Culture: Architecture, Urbanism, Identity*. Abingdon: Routledge.

Kostof, Spiro. 1991. *The city Shaped: Urban Patterns and Meanings Through History*. Boston: Little Brown.
Koyagi, Mikiya. 2015. "The Vernacular Journey: Railway Travelers in Early Pahlavi Iran." *International Middle East Studies* 47: 745–763.
Lamparkos, Michele. 2014. "The Idea of the Historic City." *Change Over Time (Project Muse)* 4 (1): 8–38.
Lieto, Laura. 2015. "Cross-Border Mythologies: The Problem With Traveling Planning Ideas." *Planning Theory* 14 (2): 115–129.
Madanipour, Ali. 1998. *Tehran: The Making of a Metropolis*. Wiley.
—. 2006. "Urban Planning and Development in Tehran." *Cities* 23 (6): 433–438.
Makki, Hosein. 1982. *Tarikhche Bist Saaleie Iran*. Vol. 4. Tehran: Kavian.
Mamdani, Mahmood. 1996. *Citizen and Subject*. Princeton: Princeton University Press.
Matin-Asgari, Afshin. 2012. "The Pahlavi Era Iranian Modernity in Global Context." In *The Oxford Handbook of Iranian History*, by Touraj Daryaee, 346–364. Oxford: Oxford Handbooks Online.
McFarland, Stephen L. 1985. "Anatomy of an Iranian Political Crowd: The Tehran Bread Riot of December 1942." *International Journal of Middle East Studies* 17 (1): 51–65.
McFarlane, Colin. 2011. *Learning the City: Knowledge and Trans Local Assemblage*. London: Wiley-Blackwell.
McQuire, Scott. 2008. *The Media City: Media, Architecture, and Urban Space*. London: SAGE Publications.
Mehan, Asma. 2017. "Urban Branding Politics in Post-Fordist Cities: The Case of Turin." *The Fourth Valletta 2018 Annual International Conference, Living Spaces, Livable Spaces: Place Making and Identity*. Valletta, Malta: The Valletta 2018 Foundation.
—. 2019. "The Challenge of Comparative Urbanism in Post Fordist Cities: the Cases of Turin and Detroit." *Contour Journal* (EPFL University) (4 (Comparing Habitats)): 1–14.
—. 2022. "Petroleum Industry Museums in Iran." *TICCIH Bulletin* 96: 27–28.
Mehan, Asma, and Miriam Bodino. 2018. "Il Louvre a Teheran, in Equilibrio Tra Cultura e Politica." *Il Giornale dell'Architettura*, 1–3. Torino, Italia: Società Editrice Umberto Allemandi & C.
Mehan, Asma, and Rowena Abdul Razak. 2022. "LA FUTURA EREDITÀ ENERGETICA NEL GOLFO PERSICO E NEL MAR CINESE MERIDIONALE: IL CASO DEL PATRIMONIO PETROLIFERO IN IRAN E MALESIA." *Labor Est* 1 (24): 57–63.
Mehan, Asma, and Mostafa Behzadfar. 2018. "The Forgotten Legacy: Oil Heritage Sites in Iran." *CONGRESO XVII TICCIH—CHILE (Patrimonio Industrial: Entendiendo El Pasado, Haciendo El Futuro Sostenible)*, 897–900. Santiago: Universidad Central de Chile, Santiago.
Milani, Abbas. 2004. *Lost Wisdom: Rethinking Modernity in Iran*. Washington: Mage Publishers.

Morris, Neil. 2016. "Tehran (Teheran)." In *Dictionary Plus Social Sciences.* Oxford: Oxford University Press.

Nasr, Joe, and Mrercedes Volait. 2003. *Urbanism: Imported or Exported?* Chichester: Wiley.

Nijman, Jan. 2015. "The Theoretical Imperative of Comparative Urbanism: A Commentary on 'Cities Beyond Compare'? by Jamie Peck." *Regional Studies* 49 (1).

Paccoud, Antoine. 2017. "Planning Law, Power, and Practice: Haussmann in Paris (1853–1870)." *Planning Perspectives* 31 (3): 341–361.

Parkinson, John R. 2012. *Democracy and Public Space: The Physical Sites of Democratic Performance.* Oxford: Oxford University Press.

Rabinow, Paul. 1989. "Governing Morocco: Modernity and Difference." *International Journal of Urban and Regional Research* 13 (1): 32–46.

Rahdari, Amir, Asma Mehan, and Asma Malekpourasl. 2019. "Sustainable Real Eastate in the Middle East: Challenges and Future Trends." In *Sustainable Real Estate: Multidisciplinary Approaches to an Evolving System*, by Thomas Walker, Cary Krosinsky, Lisa N. Hasan and Stéfanie D. Kibsey, 403–426. Cham, Switzerland: Palgrave Macmillan.

Robinson, Jennifer. 2011. "Cities in a World of Cities: The Comparative Gesture." *International Journal of Urban and Regional Research (IJURR)* 35 (1): 1–23.

Rosner, Victoria. 2005. *Modernism and the Architecture of Private Life.* New York: Columbia University Press.

Safamanesh, Kamran, and Behrouz Monadizadeh. 1999. "Changes in Architecture and Urbansim between 1920–1941." *Second Congress of Iranian Architectural History* 247–273.

Schorske, Carl Emil. 1981. *Fin De Siècle Vienna: Politics and Culture.* Cambridge: CUP Archive.

Scott, James C. 1998. *Seeing Like a State.* Yale: Yale University Press.

Shahri, Jafar. 1993. *The Old Tehran.* Vol. 1. Tehran: Moen Book Publishing House.

Shirazian, Reza. 2013. "Two Approaches to the Expansion of Tehran (in Farsi)." *Architecture and Culture* 52: 6–10.

Takmilhomayoun, Naser. 2000. *Taarikh-e Farhangi Va Ejtemaei-e Tehran.* Vol. 2. Tehran: Cultural Research Center.

Unger, R.M. 1998. *Democracy Realized: the Progressive Alternative.* London: Verso.

Ward, Kevin. 2008. "Editorial—Toward a Comparative (re)turn in Urban Studies? Some Reflections." *Urban Geography* 29: 405–410.

Ward, Stephen V. 2003. "Re-Examining the International Diffusion of Planning." In *Urban Planning in a Changing World: The Twentieth Century Experience*, by Robert Freestone, 40–60. London: E and FN Spon.

Wilber, Donald. 1975. *Riza Shah: the Resurrection and Reconstruction of Iran.* New York: Mazda Pub.

Wilson, Elizabeth. 1991. *The Sphinx in the City: Urban Life, the Control of Disorder, and Women*. Berkeley and Los Angeles: University of California Press.

—. 2003. *Adorned in Dreams: Fashion and Modernity*. Rutgers: Rutgers University Press.

Zender, Heidi Brevik. 2015. *Fashioning Spaces: Mode and Modernity in Late Nineteenth Century Paris*. Toronto: University of Toronto Press.

3 City of Power Reasons

Introduction: "Towards a New Architecture"

The very primitive idea of this chapter is grounded in the formulations of Le Corbusier's final chapter in the book "Towards a New Architecture." In "Architecture ou Révolution," Le Corbusier deduced that "Revolution" could be avoided through the scientific application of innovative techniques. This optimistic faith in the rational efficiency of scientific progress is usually classified as the "typical" feature of the modern movement, even in a different context. This angle helps to analyze Tehran's utopian planning schemes. Starting from the nineteenth century, the historical developments in Iran show a dramatic transition from a feudal social formation to a capitalist one (Halliday 1979; Mehan 2017a).

Architecture has always been used to mediate forms of political power to propagate political ideologies to society (Vale 2008). During the post-World War Two period, the immediate need for massive construction in Tehran resulted in new planning and design processes. It paved the way for the rapid implementation of urban political projects. The urban megaprojects depicted a different future for the city (Mehan 2019).

It is important to note that each utopian ideals, values, norms, and perceptions would respond differently to the various political and cultural contexts. In this regard, if we consider utopia as an ideal urban form, here the main question arises: what is an ideal urban form, according to whom and by what standards? In order to responding to these questions in the global south context, a much more deep, nuanced, and dialectic understanding of urban interventions is required (Picon 2013). Here, the focus will be on Tehran's urban planning as the essential link between architectural emancipation, state-power ideologies, bureaucratic rationality, and transcending urban life.

DOI: 10.4324/9781003140795-4

This chapter clarifies the association between totalizing state-power and megalomaniac projects through the semantic (re)readings of Tehran's urban projects. It is important to note that every form of politics has a spatial narrative style. So, spatial visions can build the imaginary narrations of political culture.

Utopia and heterotopia are the terms that have major significance in the discourse on space, culture, and politics. The links between architecture and utopia have become more tenuous since orthodox modernist architecture and urbanism was described as utopian, not less so. Indeed, they are a wide range of different interpretations. As Kroeber (1992) puts it, the defining feature of modernism is its disenchantment with utopian narratives (1). The value orientation of a utopian community can be reflected through architecture and the built environment. In this way, architecture and the built environment can reflect the social order of society. According to Grosz (2001), utopic visions are "represented as the cessation of becoming, the overcoming of problems, a calm and ongoing resolution" (139). For Green (1993), "the architectural elements of Utopian communities include boundaries (edges), gateways, paths, gathering nodes, landmarks, and landscaped gardens. These elements can be viewed as reflections of Utopian philosophy and, once built, designated or planted, influence the social behavior that occupies their domain" (Green 1993, 9). Since most utopias are contained in some manner by boundaries that have significant social functions, the conceptualization of socio-political concepts is critical in identifying society.

For Rajchman, to experience the heterotopic moments of invention, we need to disengage from the taken-for-granted historical construction. The heterotopic moments are as yet unknown; they are not possible but actual. They act as thinking otherwise, reclaiming Foucault's account of inhabiting the uninhabitable, the heterotopia (Rajchman 1991, 162). During the recent century, various political events in Tehran emphasize the necessity of further discussions to analyze the relationship between planning ideas, utopian urban projects, heterotopia, and revolution. The ruling power symbolically uses the urban space as a tool to exercise its authority to declare and enact political intention (Dovey 1999; Sudjic 2011). This struggle has been reflected in two revolutions and numerous protest movements, which often occur in Tehran and other major cities of Iran (Mehan 2017b; 2017c; 2017d). This research shows that the architectural paradigms encompass comprehensive and critical visions of social transformation—of the politics, society, and culture. It will interrogate the relationship between urban utopias, heterotopias, and revolutions. It asks whether utopian speculation can be considered an effective political strategy. It is roughly concerned with the ways political power is inscribed in Tehran's primary urban design and planning interventions in the second Pahlavi period.

Architecture Ou Révolution

In 1923, Le Corbusier's book *Vers une architecture* bore the title *Architecture ou Révolution* as the subject of the book's crucial final chapter. The book ends with the following paragraph: "Society violently desires one thing that it will obtain or that it will not. Everything lies in that; everything will depend on the effort and attention paid to these alarming symptoms. Architecture or Revolution; Revolution can be avoided" (LeCorbusier 1989, 269). The final statement, "Architecture can prevent Revolution," seems challenging. In better words, Le Corbusier, in common with many modern movement architects, perceived architecture as an overtly political apparatus in combating social unrest. He assumed that "revolution" could be avoided through the scientific application of innovative techniques and modern architecture like mass housing and urban planning that would drive architecture to prevent social discontent (McLeod 2010). For Fredric Jameson (1985), "he saw the construction and the constitution of new spaces as the most revolutionary act, and one that could 'replace' the narrowly political revolution of the mere seizure of power" (71).

According to Leach (2004), Le Corbusier spoke of avoiding political "revolution" since he recognized the possibility of a "revolution" in architecture that would go beyond political issues. In this definition, architecture is the primary product of the beginning of a different society. Jameson (2004) also observes: "it is difficult enough to imagine any radical political program today without the conception of systemic otherness, of an alternate society, which only the idea of a utopia seems to keep alive, however feebly" (36). Similarly, Simone Brott (2013) clarifies that "the conception of Modernism as a utopian project of social redemption" is the very fundamental belief in "Architecture or Revolution." This rather optimistic conception of modernism as a utopian project is usually classified as the "typical" feature of the modern movement, emphasizing the social role of architecture. So, could architecture prevent revolution?

If we really speak the modern architectural language, there are two possibilities for finding us. We will be allowed to express ourselves freely, or we will have to demolish the obstacles that prevent us from doing so, we will have to fight censorship.

(Zevi 1978, 57)

According to Zevi, the modern language of architecture is a "Revolutionary" weapon that is explosive by virtue of architecture. In other words, we have to fight against capitalist or socialist societies that place obstacles and censorship and real estate speculation in the way of modern expression. We have to cause a revolution and collectivize the use of land. The society that Zevi envisages is collective, free, and democratic. In general, the social condition is used to reflect a philosophy of historical progress based on the idea of a golden age in the past (paradise lost) and an ideal state in the future (utopia) (Tournikiotis 1999, 223). The revolutionary character of modern architecture takes on a purely utopian dimension in the reintegration of buildings, cities, and landscapes (Tournikiotis 1999, 59).

For Picon (2013), the excessive desire for reconciliation is the fundamental flaw in ambitious modern architecture projects. In response to the question of the relative "utopian-ness" of modern architecture, Coleman (2012) declares: "The largely conventional view is to see in modern architecture something of the stirrings of a revolution of a Marxist sort, which is also supposedly the core of its utopian aspiration and ultimate failure" (341). It is essential to note that utopias are critical in that they challenge the perception of the present society by considering a wide range of possible solutions to social problems. They split reality into a series of competing political projects. One person's utopia is another's dystopia (Bauman 1976, 10–37). Similarly, Tafuri emphasized the political character of the critique of modern architecture: "Just as it is not possible to find a political economy based on a class, so one cannot anticipate a class architecture (an architecture for a liberated society); what is possible is the introduction of class criticism into architecture" (Tafuri 1976; 1980). For Tafuri, the utopian nature of modern architecture is related to capitalist values (Mehan and Vaghefi 2018). In this interpretation, we can consider urban elements as "governmental apparatus" and the means to test "the political instrumentality of architecture." Therefore, "the city is the most explicit index of power relationship" (Aureli 2011, 32–37).

Architecture and Utopia

The connection between utopian thought and the city has been particularly part of dreams of spatial transformation and social process. The classical utopias were homogenous in conception. The modern post-war urban utopias are hopeful, rational, non-conflictual, dependent on dignity, and one confirmed truth and pure idealism (Siebers 1994, 21–22). The utopian urban visions expressed a desire for radical change that engaged directly with current spatial and social relations. They reveal much about the present human condition. The radical models of an ideal society are a powerful mechanism for identifying societal problems. The utility of utopia as an effective political medium clarifies and transcends the goals of mainstream political theory. However, the utopian "scientific" understanding of the present and the future had been associated with the performance of totalitarian regimes (Sarakemsky 1993). According to Heynen (2002):

> All of the criticisms that modern architecture has had to endure since the 1960s, the one of utopianism has apparently had the most impact. It seems that, by now, almost everybody is convinced that modern architecture's utopian ambition was its most harmful attribute. Its utopian aspirations are usually seen as completely bound up with paternalistic, not to say totalitarian attitudes, and are for that reason discredited and put aside.
>
> (382)

The French Revolution significantly impacted modern utopian thinking (Sarakemsky 1993). In the late nineteenth and early twentieth centuries, broad utopian approaches emerged in response to urban problems. In 1898, Ebenezer Howard published a book entitled "To-Morrow: A Peaceful Path to Real Reform." A revised edition appeared four years later under "Garden Cities of To-Morrow." Howard presented the garden city as a new spatial form through which new social arrangements and eventually new social order could develop (Pinder 2005). Howard emphasized the need for scientific systems of railways, canals, and reservoirs in the networks and routes of his depicted "social city." This circulation and constant movement became an essential urban policy during the nineteenth century (Pinder 2005, 48).

During the twentieth century, utopian urban projects mostly but not inclusively manifested in the visionary works of Howard, Gruen, Wright, and Le Corbusier. These utopian concepts emerged from visionary planners such as Victor Gruen (1903–1980) and his "Metropolis of Tomorrow." In *The Heart of Our Cities: The Urban Crisis; Diagnoses and Cure* (1964), Gruen depicted *the Metropolis of Tomorrow* with the metro center surrounded by ten towns, each town center surrounded by four communities, each community center by five neighborhoods. Each city is like a cell in this cellular city, with a town center acting as a nucleus. This clustered super organism is called "Metropolis of Tomorrow" based on Gruen's model inspired by Ebenezer Howard's "Garden Cities of To-Morrow" (Wakeman 2016, 280).

In the early twentieth century, the utopian visions of cities associated with the modern movement aimed to confront urban problems. Anthony Vilder (2011) employs the Foucauldian notion of panopticons, identifying the blind spots of current spatial analysis to consider the Enlightenment fear of darkness and the political role of transparency and Utopia in modern architecture (36). In this definition, Foucault's panopticon operates as an architectural controlling device serving spatial surveillance.

During the 1920s and 1930s, utopian urbanism was envisioned by Le Corbusier and the modern ideal city forms. Like Howard, Le Corbusier shared concerns on "circulation" and sought an alternative in "vertical garden" cities. Throughout the utopian concepts of *Ville Radieuse* (Radiant City or Machine City), Le Corbusier aimed to create a social and economic revolution with the employment of utopian urban orders. In this manner, Le Corbusier's formulation "Architecture or Revolution" emphasized changing architecture and urban space as a radical act that extends into the heart of social, cultural, and political conditions (Pinder 2005, 64). As a result of these new urban interventions, "A vision of a new world is born: a fully integrated world of high-rise towers surrounded by vast expanses of grass and open space-linked by aerial superhighways, serviced by subterranean garages and shopping arcades (Berman 1983, 167)."

During the 1950s and late 1960s, the culmination of vicious factors such as urban sprawl, increased use of automobiles, separation of urban functions, and the problems of the inner city led the planners to imagine a new utopian city image on an international scale. Victor Gruen (1973) used the term "Anti-City" to describe the "rise of the uni-functional center" (the title of the fourth chapter of Gruen's book: *Centers for the Urban Environment*) and the "downfall of Urbanism" (86). Gruen believed that "using cars in modern cities meant tearing the urban tissue apart with streets, expressways, freeways and parking lots." Gruen sought to solve the problem by separating those functions dependent on large quantities of vehicular traffic from others, which depend on a smaller amount. In a better word, certain urban parts like working tasks of all types, shopping functions, and significant places of assembly have to be separated from residential functions (Gruen 1973, 85–86).

For presenting the suburban labyrinth, Victor Gruen's definition of "Enforced Mobility" tried to illustrate graphically in a simplified schematic way. This kind of "Involuntary Mobility" acts concerning three typical middle-class families' units (the lower-middle-class family/the middle-middle-class family/the upper-middle-class family). Gruen (1973) concluded that introducing one multifunctional center would dissolve the labyrinth effect (87–88). He argued that urban life and sustainability would improve through an international system of medium-sized, dense, urbane, and cellular metropolises (Hill 1992).

Some persistent proposals for envisioning the ideal city affected Gruen's utopian planning: Le Corbusier's Ville Radieuse (Radiant City or Machine City) and Ville Contemporarie as well as Frank Lloyd Wright's unbuilt suburban utopia: Broadacre City (Known as *the Disappearing City* or *the Living City*). In the Broadacre City project, Wright deliberately tried to promote the values of the rich and open family life by eliminating small, separate rooms and creating open space centered around the hearth (Fishman 1982, 111).

For Gruen (1964), Le Corbusier's Radiant City, proposed in 1925, had destroyed any hope of accommodating the car, featured a central city composed of skyscrapers (178). Frank Lloyd Wright's Broadacre City, also referred to as the "Living City," featured a central city composed of skyscrapers and glorified the automobile's use as a means of transportation. Gruen labels Wright's Broadacre as the "Anti-City," a significant city that served as an employment center, surrounded by rings of residential garden cities linked to the central employment center through highways. In the same period, Gruen was also influenced by various supporters of the organic planning tradition like Ebenezer Howard (1902), Lewis Mumford (1961), and Jane Jacobs (1961) (Hill 1992, 315). Embracing Wright's garden city motif, Victor Gruen's "Metropolis of Tomorrow" centered on the idea of cluster planning, influenced by a linear version of Ebenezer Howard's Social City with satellite garden cities around the metropolis core (Ward 2016). Wakeman (2016) argues that Gruen's desire to restore the sense of community was influenced by *Ebenezer Howard, Lewis Mumford,* and *Jane Jacobs* (Figures 3.1 and 3.2 A and B).

Planning "Metropolis of To-Morrow"

In the post-war period, the confrontation between the East and the West polarized the dissemination of architecture and planning concepts. The export of "Modernism" and its adaptations to the conditions of "Third World" from Socialist and Capitalist countries

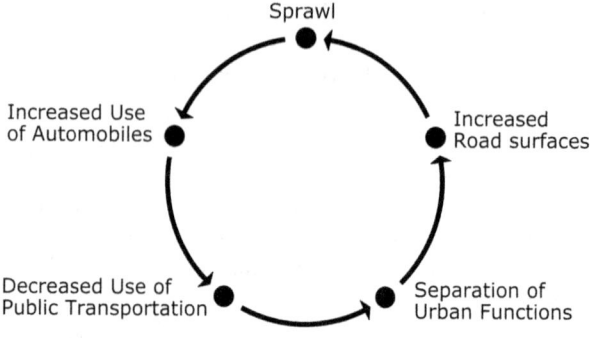

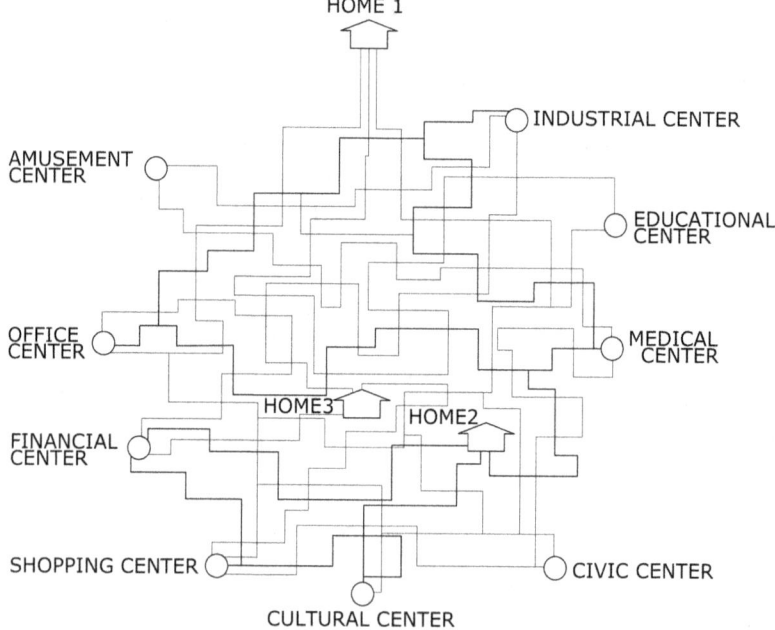

Figure 3.1 The vicious circle (up) and the suburban labyrinth (down).

Source: Victor Gruen, *Centers for the Urban Environment* (Los Angeles, Van Nostrand Reinhold Company, 1973), 86 and 87.

introduced the new paradigms of reconstruction and resettlement policies that create new urban identities in these countries (Mehan, 2017e). In cold war politics, urban planning was considered a powerful instrument. The export of architecture and planning functioned as

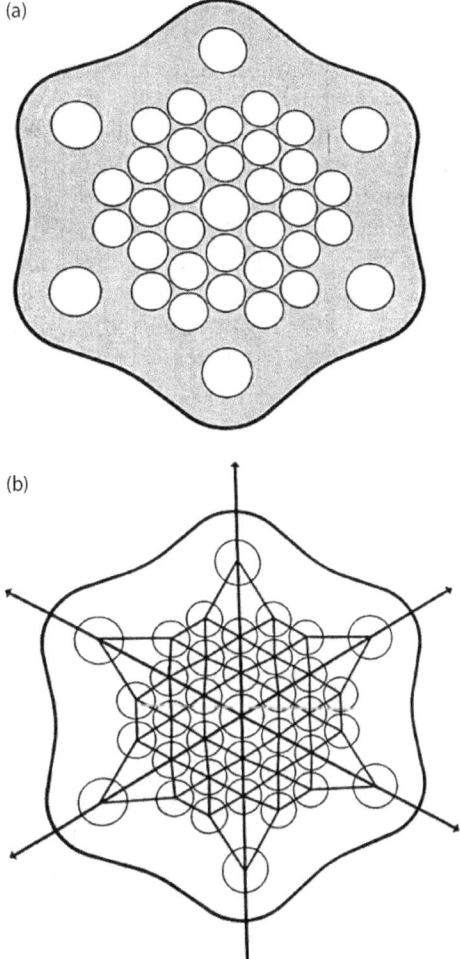

Figure 3.2 (A) Abstract model of an urban organism: relationship between green areas and urban subunits. (B) Abstract model of an urban organism: public transportation.

Source: Victor Gruen, *Centers for the Urban Environment* (Los Angeles, Van Nostrand Reinhold Company, 1973), 208 and 209.

a political apparatus by non-government aid organizations, philanthropic foundations, corporations, and individual professionals.

During the early 1960s, the Kennedy Administration was urging its allies in the third world to carry out necessary social reforms (by using aid as leverage) to prevent popular discontent and enhance the dominant ideology of "modernism" (Root 2008, 125). Consequently, beginning in 1961, the king of Iran had initiated a series of land reforms and national modernization projects entitled "White Revolution" or the "Revolution of Shah and People," which included social, political, and economic reforms. This series of reforms was termed "white" for their implementation without bloodshed (Madanipour 1998). Similarly, Ford Foundation described its urban planning projects in "Third World" countries as "white bread," the innocent, soft bread that everybody likes with no particular taste (Provoost 2007).

In 1968, a significant piece of legislation, the Urban Development and Renewal Act, enabled the municipality to implement Tehran's Comprehensive Plan (Figure 3.3). The plan, which was eventually approved in 1970 by the city council and the High Council for Town Planning and Architecture, defined two axes for the city: the pre-existing north-south axis and the new east-west axis, guided by a new superhighway and subway network. The planning of the Master Plan, which was supposed to take Tehran forward by 25 years, was entrusted to Victor Gruen. He worked with the Iranian architect Abdol Aziz Farman Farmaian under the direction of the Iranian city planner *Fereydun Ghaffari* and Iranian Mayor *Gholam Reza Nikpei*. The planning horizon was 1991 when the new Tehran would reach its maximum extent. Tehran's Comprehensive Plan integrated all the 1960s' American city elements, such as the separation of functions, highways, suburbs, shopping centers, and housing areas (Madanipour 1998) (Figure 3.4).

Tehran's master plan envisaged a class-segregated and socially-segregated society that denoted some ideals of bourgeoisie freedom (Emami 2014). Wakeman (2016) argues that the development of small new town projects in the late 1950s and early 1960s was based on strict social segregation. She added: "Kuy-e Narmak northeast of the capital for middle-income residents, Nazi-Abad for working-class families and the northern garden city of Tehran Pars for the upper classes." She added, "critics argued that the plan looked shockingly like Los Angeles, strewn with highways and dominated by development interests. It was put into practice by a combination of American companies and Western-minded elites, many of whom (such as *Abdol-Aziz Farman-Farmaian*) had studied in England or at the Ecole des Beaux-Arts in Paris and also worked in the United States (like *Fereydoon Ghaffari*)" (Wakeman 2016). For creating the almost American metropolis, high-rise and mid-rise residential buildings became one of the main typologies that the Master Plan proposed (Zareh 2010). In 1968, Rahman Golzar and Jordan Gruzen collaborated with

City of Power Reasons 63

Figure 3.3 Master Plan of Tehran prepared for the Shah of Iran, 1967.
Source: Jeffrey M. Hardwick. *Mall Maker: Victor Gruen, Architect of an American Dream* (Pennsylvania: University of Pennsylvania Press, 2004), 222.

Victor Gruen to design the biggest high-rise residential complex in the Middle Eastern region at the time: Ekbatan Residential Complex in the western edge of Tehran along with the new international Airport of the time—Mehrabad Airport—and, the grand-scale project of

64 *City of Power Reasons*

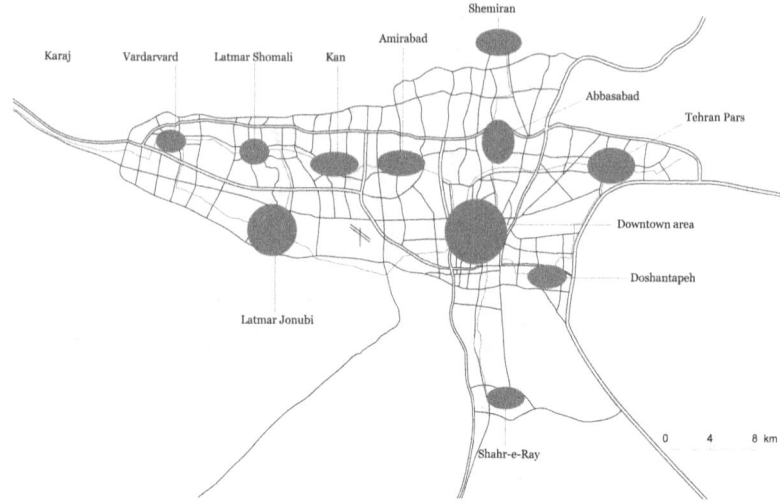

Figure 3.4 Urban districts proposed by the Tehran Comprehensive Plan.
Source: Llewelyn-Davies International, Shahestan Pahlavi (1976), Book I, 30.

Shahyad (now Azadi) Square as the new gateway of the city (Mehan and Mehan 2020). This project manifested the utopian nature of modern architecture, reflecting capitalist values (Mehan 2015; 2016) (Figure 3.5).

During this period, the new developments supported by the oil boom of the 1970s were built in different forms to constitute an expanding metropolis. In these years, the king introduced himself as a sincere "democrat" determined to "modernize" a highly "traditional society" (Abrahamian 1982). In a press conference in 1971, Shah explained his "Great Civilization" comparable to Mussolini's "Olympiad of Civilization":

> I think that we can say very firmly and with absolute certainty that Iran will not only become an industrial nation but in my assessment will, in 12 years' time, enter what we say the era of the Great Civilization. The era of the Great Civilization, for those who are interested to know, is a kind of welfare state, where everybody from birth until death will enjoy every kind of social insurances.
>
> (Ansari 2003, 172)

With the dominant ideology of "nationalism," Mohammad Reza Shah's utopic view toward Iran as a "Great Civilization" and his

Figure 3.5 Ekbatan Residential Complex.
Source: Atlas de Téhéran métropole, Vol. 1. La terre et les homes (2005).

"megalomaniac delusion of Grandeur" captured in this national slogan: "God-King-Homeland." Mozaffari (2014), in his book "Forming National Identity in Iran," introduced the very notion of this slogan as the connection between monarchy, nationalism, and national identity (28–29). In the book *Mission for my Country,* Mohammad Reza Shah wrote:

Most of the readers of this book will have studied Roman history, but our empire was flourishing centuries before that of Rome, and it was in fact we who showed that it was possible to govern and administer on such a large scale.

(Pahlavi 1961)

According to Grigor (2014), the new Pahlavi regime furthered the pre-existing "dialectical and ambivalent relationship developed between artists and architects at the service of the state and the centralist state that founded institutions intending to produce the professional middle class" wherein "high art stood as a signifier of utopian modernity" (18–19). The second "International Congress of Architecture" with the theme of "Toward a Quality of Life" was held at Persepolis in 1974 in response to the challenges posed by increasing oil revenues. Some of the well-known architects and planners of that time: Oswald Mathias Ungers, Constantinos A. Doxiadis, Georges Candilis, Balkrishna V. Doshi, Moshe Safdi, Richard Buckminster Fuller, Kenzo Tange, Fumiohiko Maki, I. M. Pei, James Stirling, Hans Hollein, and many more were invited to Persepolis, the old capital, to showcase their new conceptions about Tehran (Zareh 2010). Madanipour assesses the ekistics planning models in the case of the Tehran Action Plan issued by Doxiadis Associates in 1972 as the last modernist ambitions before the advent of laissez-faire urban development (Madanipour 2010; Theodosis 2015).

In 1973, the royal government of Iran invited two prominent architects of the time, Louis Kahn and Kenzo Tange, to suggest a plan for the National Center of Tehran in the Abbas Abad Hills. The exceptional location of Abbas Abad at the intersection of the two main axes of the future city: the preexisting north-south axis and the new east-west axis based on the Tehran Comprehensive Plan of 1968 made it the best location for building a national center at the very heart of metropolis (Emami 2014). On the periphery of the sketch, Kahn referred to the *Palazzo dei Congressi*, his unbuilt concept for a bridge-shaped congress hall in Venice. Kahn also indicated that he saw the plaza as a meeting place of the East and the West. However, Kahn's death marked the end of this promising collaboration. Shortly after, the king commissioned the British office Llewelyn-Davis International to take up the project.

In 1975, a short essay published by New York Times magazine entitled "Teheran Planning One of the World's Largest Plazas," which is planned to be larger than Red Square in Moscow, called "Shah and Nation Square." This new gigantic urban plaza was part of the ambitious urban project, known as "Shahestan Pahlavi" or Place of Shah (king) in Abbas Abad hills of Tehran by the planners of the English new town Milton Keynes together with the American firm of Jaquelin T. Robertson (Pace 1975). This multipurpose square was a central spine of the new capitol complex containing prestigious concepts for ministry buildings, the municipality, financial institutions, commercial offices, shopping areas, housing, entertainment, recreational facilities, and a national cultural center (Figure 3.6). Although the idea was borrowed from New York's Central Park design, Jaquelin T. Robertson—the chief planner of the Llewelyn Davies international group—has emphasized traditional Iranian elements in their plans for Shahestan Pahlavi. According to Robertson, the multipurpose Shah and Nation Square (in Iranian Language Meydan-e Shah) was supposed to be wider than the famous Naghsh-e Jahan Square at Isfahan. Although this Utopian urban Plaza in the new cultural center of Tehran was never built, it is compared to the outstanding achievements of Shah Abbas in Isfahan, Pope Sixtus V in Rome, and Baron Haussmann in Paris.

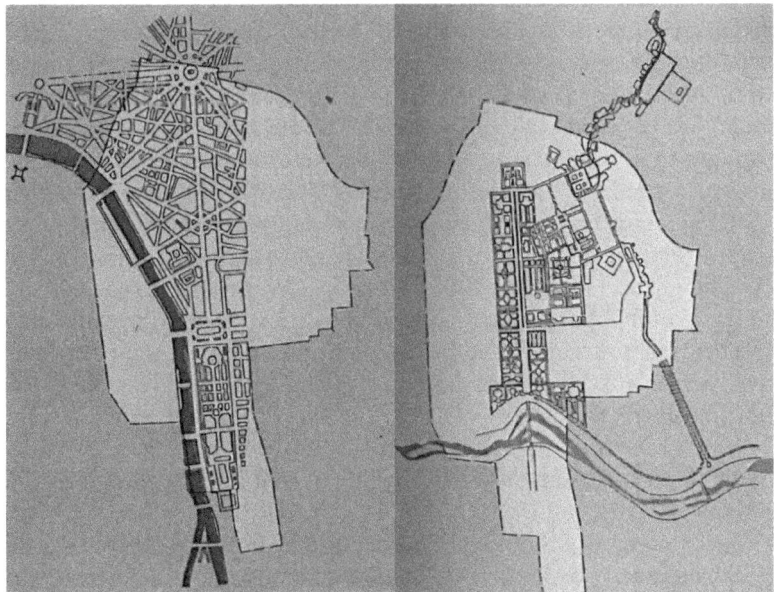

Figure 3.6 The site of Shahestan Pahlavi is large enough to contain the grand axis of Paris or the entire center of Isfahan.

Source: Llewelyn-Davies International, Shahestan Pahlavi (1976), Book I, 37

Making Heterotopia

In 1967, Michel Foucault introduced the term *heterotopia* (literally means other places), pointed to different places that interrupt the apparent normality of everyday places. According to Foucault (1984):

> There are also, probably in every culture, in every civilization, real places—places that do exist and that are formed in the very founding of society—which are something like counter-sites, a kind of effectively enacted utopia in which the real sites, all the other real sites that can be found within the culture, are simultaneously represented, contested, and inverted. Places of this kind are outside of all places, even though it may be possible to indicate their location in reality. Because these places are absolutely different from all the sites that they reflect and speak about, I shall call them, by way of contrast to utopias, heterotopias.
>
> (3)

Boyer (2008), in his book "The Many Mirrors of Foucault and Their Architectural Reflections," argues that heterotopias are "counter-discourses"—spaces of "contestation and reverberation," and "other" space. By linking the notion of another space and "thinking otherwise," Boyer (2008) questions the disciplinary thought that regulates subjectivity. So, heterotopias are ambiguous, non-totalizable, contradictory spaces (Mehan 2018). In our modern society, heterotopias are becoming very central. They can juxtapose several emplacements in a single real place that are incompatible (Dehaene and De Cauter 2008, 3–4).

The political geographer Edward Soja (1996) traces the same idea in Thirdspace, arguing that the proliferating Foucauldian approaches miss a crucial point of his thought—to challenge "conventional spatial thinking." Soja (1996) calls his alternative account, derived from Foucault's heterotopology, "the geo-history of otherness." Such a method, for Soja, acts as an envisioning of spatiality to go beyond the established (163).

Focusing on "spatial turn" in critical urban studies, Edward Soja (1989) defined "postmodernity" as the generalization of heterotopia, of the pluralistic coexistence of elements that one would "normally" think or find apart. While utopias struggle to change society with more "constructive potency" than standard political theorists offer, the production of the heterotopia is the political reaction to the dominant praxis (Goodwin and Keith 1982, 26). Foucault (1970) describes this difference as follows:

> Utopias afford consolation: although they have no real locality there is nevertheless a fantastic, untroubled region in which they are able to unfold. Heterotopias are disturbing, probably because They make it impossible to name this and that.
>
> (xix)

As Habermas (1986) puts it, "people do not fight for abstractions, but with images. Banners, symbols, and images, rhetorical speech, allegorical speech, utopia-inspired speech, in which concrete goals are conjured up before people's eyes, are indeed necessary constituents of movements which have any effect on history at all" (146). At the same time, "people always need a material basis on which to organize their autonomy against institutional power" (Castells 1983, 70).

The Shahyad (literally *In the Memory of King*) monument was built in 1971 on the 2,500th anniversary of founding the Persian Empire by the Great Cyrus. According to Grigor (2003), it is "an excellent synthesis of Roman triumphal arches, Parthian fire temples (Chahar-Taq), the Sasanian Ctesiphon Iwan, Seljuk tomb towers, Safavid muqarnas, and the various modernist architectural qualities of austerity, iconoclasm, axiality, and monumentality" (211).

The whole ethos of the 2,500th anniversary celebrations can be ascribed to this desire on behalf of the Shah's regime to display their country as genuinely outstanding in world history. It was a genuine opportunity to present Iran as "the world's center of gravity" (Shawcross 1989, 39). Similarly, a passage from a memoir published on the occasion of the Shah's coronation in 1967 expresses this sentiment: "It has been said that what Xenophon wrote of Cyrus the Great in 401 B.C. could equally well have been written of Mohammad Reza Shah Pahlavi" (Zahedi 1967, p. xvii).

In October 1971, Peter Avery (1971) contributed a chapter to the special edition of UNESCO's Courier, entitled "Iran: 'Cultural Crossroads for 2,500 Years.'" Concerning the event, Fakhreddin Azimi (2008), in his book *Quest for Democracy in Iran,* referred to the Shah's "perilous arrogance" in his presentation of a king completely out of touch with the aspirations of his people (290). Through nationalist celebration, the ruling authority seeks to gain "admiration" and "passivity" of its citizens (Podeh 2011, 21). According to Shakibi (2013), "A vital element of an ideology is a fashioned historiography that supports the regime by rooting it in the past or presenting it as the final inevitable result of historical forces" (118).

On December 12, 1978, Shahyad Square, a brand-new showcase square at the western entrance to the city, provided an open space for revolutionaries. More than 2 million people occupied the square in protest against Mohammad Reza Shah Pahlavi. Shahyad Square became available to everybody, and the crowd was claiming a revolution out of the square's public space. The square became widely known as Freedom Square after the 1978 Iranian Islamic revolution and was officially renamed after the 1978 Iranian Islamic revolution. The term in Persian for freedom, *Azadi*, has a mystical interpretation. Its ambivalent nature and the co-existence of otherwise nearly incompatible realities made Shahyad Square a "heterotopia."

Concluding Notes

This chapter reintroduced architecture and planning as the "political apparatus" for sustaining power relations and disseminating ideologies through modern planning ideas and practices. It is important to note that examining the variety of urban processes and planning politics in the "Third World" gives a comprehensive and critical introduction to the main theories that have been used to understand political changes in developing countries (Smith 2003)—considering the spatial politics of revolutionary transformation, conceptualizing connections as heterotopic allows us to appreciate their political efficacy and significance. The capitalist model as the project of building new urban formations from scratch was a response to a global discourse of modernization that viewed the rapid growth of cities in the emerging "Third World" both as an inevitable corollary of "modernity" and as a potential threat to the welfare and political stability (Daechsel 2013, 88)—rendering the importance of the complex relationship between interrelated politics in the geopolitical matrix of post-war led to a series of problematic questions on modern architectural concepts and meta-political strategies that frame social life in an oppressive frame.

This chapter depicted a subtler assessment of capitalist-inspired and utopian modernization processes in the second half of the twentieth century that influenced the paradigms of contemporary urbanization processes. Modern architecture "contains ideas, inculcates values, and serves as the tangible expressions of systems of thought" (Olsen 1986, 4). In addition, modern architecture shares a strong sense of social public responsibility in that architecture should raise the living conditions of the commons (Mehan and Mehan 2022). This research demonstrates that Modern Architecture's progressive spirit was so powerful that politicians used it to promote their ideas and national propagandas. The dominant use of public spaces during the first Pahlavi Era was for royal celebrations and representative festivals, in which people had the role of passive observance. Tehran's modernization politics and spatial transformation through utopian urban projects (directly or indirectly) created the pseudo-political nodes for active political representation.

References

Abrahamian, Ervand. 1982. *Iran between Two Revolutions*. New Jersey: Princeton University Press.
Ansari, Ali. 2003. *Modern Iran Since 1921: The Pahlavis and After*. London: Pearson Education Limited.
Aureli, Pier Vittorio. 2011. "City as Political Form, Four Archetypes of Urban Transformation." *Architectural Design* 8 (1): 32–37.
Avery, Peter. 1971. *Iran: Cultural Crossroads for 2,500 Years*. The UNESCO Courier, 4–12.
Azimi, Fakhreddin. 2008. *Quest for Democracy in Iran: A Century of Struggle Against Authoritarian Rule*. Cambridge: Harvard University Press.
Bauman, Zygmunt. 1976. *Socialism: The Active Utopia*. London: George Allen and Unwin.
Berman, Marshall. 1983. *All That Is Solid Melts into Air: The Experience of Modernity*. London: Verso.
Boyer, M. Christine. 2008. "The Many Mirrors of Foucault and Their Architectural Reflections." In *Heterotopia and the City: Public Space in a Post-Civil Society*. London: Routledge.
Brott, Simone. 2013. "Architecture Et RÉVOLUTION: Le Corbusier and the Fascist Revolution." *Thresholds* 41: 146–157.
Castells, Manuel. 1983. *The City and the Grassroots*. Berkley: University of California.
Coleman, Nathaniel. 2012. "Utopia and Modern Architecture?" *Architectural Research Quarterly* 16: 339–348.
Daechsel, Markus. 2013. "Misplaced Ekistics: Islamabad and the Politics of Urban Development in Pakistan." *South Asian History and Culture* 4 (1): 87–106.
Dehaene, Michiel, and Lieven De Cauter. 2008. *Heterotopia and the City: Public Space in a Post-Civil Society*. Routledge.
Dovey, Kim. 1999. *Framing Places: Mediating Power in Built Form*. London: Routledge.
Emami, Farshid. 2014. "Urbanism of Grandiosity: Planning a New Urban Centre for Tehran (1973–76)." *International Journal of Islamic Architecture (IJIA)* 3 (1): 69–102.

Fishman, Robert. 1982. "Urban Utopias in the Twentieth Century." In *Le Corbusier*, by Ebenezer Howard and Frank Lloyd. Wright. Cambridge: MIT Press.
Foucault, Michel. 1970. *The Order of Things: An Archeology of Human Sciences*. London and New York: Routledge.
—. 1984. "Des espaces autres," Architecture/Mouvement/Continuité; available in English as "Of Other Spaces (1967), Heterotopias," trans. Jay Miskowiec, Accessed May 27, 2020, http://foucault.info/documents/heteroTopia/foucault.heteroTopia.en.html
Green, Ernest. 1993. "The Social Functions of Utopian Architecture." *Utopian Studies* 4(3): 1–13.
Grigor, Talinn. 2003. "Of Metamorphosis: Meaning on Iranian Terms." *Third Text* 17 (3): 207–225.
—. 2014. *Contemporary Iranian Art: From the Street to the Studio*. London: Reaktin Books Ltd.
Grosz, Elizabeth. 2001. *Architecture from the Outside: Essays on Virtual and Real Space*. Cambridge, MA: MIT Press.
Gruen, Victor. 1964. *The Heart of Our Cities; the Urban Crisis: Diagnosis and Cure*. New York: Simon and Schuster.
—. 1973. *Centers for the Urban Environment: Survival of the Cities*. Los Angeles: Van Nostrand Reinhold Company.
Goodwin, Barbara, and Taylor Keith. 1982. *The Politics of Utopia: A Study in Theory and Practice*. New York: St. Martin's Press.
Jameson, Fredric. 1985. "Architecture and the Critique of Ideology." In *Architecture, Criticism, Ideology*, by Joan Ockman, 71. Princeton: Princeton Architectural Press.
—. 2004. "The Politics of Utopia." *New Left Review* 35–54.
Habermas, Jurgen. 1986. *Habermas: Autonomy and Solidarity*. London: Verso.
Halliday, Fred. 1979. *Iran: Dictatorship and Development*. New York: Penguin Books.
Heynen, Hilde. 2002. "Engaging Modernism." In *Back from Utopia: The Challenge of the Modern Movement*, by Hubert-Jan Henket and Hilde Heynen, 378–99. Rotterdam: 010 Uitgeverij.
Hill, David R. 1992. "Sustainability, Victor Gruen, and the Cellular Metropolis." *Journal of the American Planning Association* 58 (3): 312–326.
Kroeber, Karl. 1992. *Retelling/Rereading: The Fate of Storytelling in Modern Times*. New Brunswick: Rutgers University Press.
Leach, Neil. 2004. *Architecture and Revolution: Contemporary Perspectives on Central and Eastern Europe*. London and New York: Routledge.
Corbusier, Le. 1989. *Towards a New Architecture*. London: Butterworth Architecture.
Madanipour, Ali. 1998. *Tehran: The Making of a Metropolis*. London: Willey.
—. 2010. "The Limits of Scientific Planning: Doxiadis and the Tehran Action Plan." *Planning Perspective* 25 (4): 485–504.

McLeod, Mary. 2010. "Architecture and Revolution: Le Corbusier, Politics and Architecture 1930–1942." *The City as a Project.*
Mehan, Asma. 2015. *Architecture for Revolution: Democracy and Public Space.* Edinburgh: Graduate Student Research Forum, Society of Architectural Historians of Great Britain (SAHGB).
—. 2016. "Urban Regeneration: A Comprehensive Strategy for Achieving Social Sustainability in Historical Public Squares," SGEM International Multidisciplinary Scientific Conference on Social Sciences and Arts (ISBN: 978-619-7105-54-4), volume 2 (pp. 862–868), Czech Republic, Prague.
—. 2017a. "Tabula Rasa" Planning: Creative Destruction and Building a New Urban Identity in Tehran." *Journal of Architecture and Urbanism* 41 (3): 210–220.
—. 2017b. "Manifestation of Modernity in Iranian Public Squares: Baharestan Square (1826–1978)." *International Journal of Heritage Architecture* 1 (3): 411–420.
—. 2017c. "Manifestation of Power: Toopkhaneh Square, Tehran." *Spaces & Flows: An International Journal of Urban & Extra Urban Studies* 8 (2): 77–88.
—. 2017d. "In razing its modernist buildings, Iran is erasing its past western influence", published online in The Conversation Media Group (Global Pilot), ISSN: 2201-5639.
—. 2017e. "Emerging Metropolis: Politics of Planning in Tehran during Cold War", Cold War at the Crossroads: 194X-98X Symposium, Department of Architecture and Urban Studies (DASTU), Milano, Politecnico di Milano, Italy.
—. 2018. "Making Heterotopia: Azadi Square as Palimpsest of Political Memory", 33rd Annual Middle East History & Theory Conference (MEHAT), The University of Chicago, Chicago, Illinois, USA.
—. 2019. "Creating New Urban Identities: Politics of Planning in 'Third World' During the Cold War." In *International Congress Colonial and Postcolonial Landscapes, Architecture, Cities, Infrastructures*, 125–126. Lisbon, Portugal: Calouste Gulbenkian Foundation.
Mehan, Asma, and Iman Vaghefi 2018. دقن یا یدئولوژی معماری در اندیشه ی مانفردو تافوری (Manfredo Tafuri's Critique of Architectural Ideology). *FAZA VA DIALECTIC* 7.
Mehan, Asma, and Mahziar Mehan. 2020. "Housing as Politics: The Case of Tehran", in *Spaces for Living Spaces for Sharing*, by Simona Canepa, 56–65. Siracusa, Italy: LetteraVentidue Edizioni.
—. 2022. "Conceptualizing the Urban Commons", in *The Palgrave Encyclopedia of Urban and Regional Futures*, by Robert Bears, 1–4. Cham, Switzerland: Palgrave Macmillan.
Mozaffari, Ali. 2014. "Forming National Identity in IRAN: The Idea of Homeland Derived from Ancient Persian and Islamic Imaginations of Place." *Excerpt From: Ali Mozaffari. "Forming National Identity in Iran."* New York: I.B. Tauris & Co Ltd.

Olsen, Donald J. 1986. *The City as a Work of Art: London, Paris, Vienna*. New Heaven: Yale University Press.
Pace, Eric. 1975. "Teheran Planning One of the World's Largest Plazas." *The New York Times Online Archive*. 09 1. Accessed August 28, 2016. https://issuu.com/perspectivemagazineberkeley/docs/perspective_spring_2019
Pahlavi, Mohammad Reza Shah. 1961. *Mission for My Country*. London: Hutchinson.
Picon, Antoine. 2013. "Learning from Utopia: Contemporary Architecture and the Quest for Political and Social Relevance." *Journal of Architectural Education* 67 (1): 17–23.
Pinder, David. 2005. *Visions of the City*. Edinburgh: Edinburgh University Press.
Provoost, Michelle. 2007. "New Towns on the Cold War Frontier: How Modern Urban Planning Was Exported as an Instrument in the Battle for the Developing World." *Crimson Architectural Historians*. https://www.crimsonweb.org/spip.php?article47.
Podeh, Elie. 2011. *The Politics of National Celebrations in the Arab Middle East*. Cambridge: Cambridge University Press.
Rajchman, John. 1991. *Philosophical Events: Essays of the 80's*. New York: Columbia University Press.
Root, Hilton L. 2008. *Alliance Curse: How America Lost the Third World*. Washington: The Brookings Institution.
Sarakemsky, Ivor. 1993. "Utopia as Political Theory, Politikon: South African Journal of Political Studies." *Politikon: South African Journal of Political Studies* 20 (2): 111–125.
Shakibi, Zhand. 2013. "Pahlavism: The Ideologization of Monarchy in Iran." *Politics, Religion, and Ideology* 14 (1).
Shawcross, William. 1989. *The Shah's Last Ride*. London: Chatto and Windus.
Siebers, Tobin. 1994. *Heterotopia: Postmodern Utopia and Body Politics*. Ann Arbor: University of Chicago Press.
Smith, Brian C. 2003. *Understanding Third World Politics: Theories of Political Change and Development*. Indiana: Indiana University Press.
Soja, Edward. 1989. *Postmodern Geographies: The Reassertion of Space in Critical Social Theory*. London: Verso.
—. 1996. *Thirdspace: Journeys to Los Angeles and Other Real-and-Imagined Places*. Cambridge, Massachusetts: Blackwell.
Sudjic, Deyan. 2011. *The Edifice Complex: The Architecture of Power*. London: Routledge.
Tafuri, Manfredo. 1976. *Architecture and Utopia; Design and Capitalist Development*. Massachusetts: The MIT Press.
—. 1980. *Theories and History of Architecture*. First English language edition. Translated by Giorgio Verrecchia. London: Harper and Row Publishers.
Theodosis, Lefteris. 2015. *Victory Over Chaos? Constantinos A. Doxiadis and Ekistics 1945–1975*. Barcelona: Universitat Politècnica de Catalunya.
Tournikiotis, Panayotis. 1999. *The Histography of Modern Architecture*. Cambridge: The MIT Press.

Vale, Lawrence. 2008. *Architecture, Power, and National Identity*. London and New York: Routledge.
Vilder, Anthony. 2011. "Transparency and Utopia: Constructing the Void from Pascal to Foucault". In *The Scenes of the Street and Other Essays*. New York: The Monacelli Press.
Wakeman, Rosemary. 2016. *Practicing Utopia: An Intellectual History of the New Town Movement*. Chicago and London: University of Chicago Press.
Ward, Tory. 2016. *The Gruen Effect In partnership with Portland State University and the International Council of Museums' Committee for the Collections and Activities of Museums of Cities (CAMOC)*. Accessed August 27, 2016. http://www.museumofthecity.org/project/the-gruen-effect/.
Zahedi, Ardeshir. 1967. "Memoir of His Imperial Majesty Mohammad Reza Shah Pahlavi, Shahanshah of Iran." In *Bibliography of Iran*, by Geoffrey Handley-Taylor. London: SFU Library.
Zareh, Vesta Nele. 2010. "An (Almost) All American City - The Vision and Legacy of the Tehran Comprehensive Plan." In *the Emerging Asian City: Its Traditions, Tensions & Transformations*, by Vinakak Bahrne, 139–147. California: California University Press.
Zevi, Bruno. 1978. *The Modern Language of Architecture*. Translated by Ronald Storm and William A. Packer. Seattle: University of Washington Press.

4 Radical Urbanism

Conceptualizing the Radical Urbanism

Cities have always been arenas of political and social conflicts. The struggle for control of public space is an ambivalent mode of politicizing and appropriating the urban space. As Lefebvre (1991) suggests, space is produced through social relations and political structure. Rather than a mere physical form, Lefebvre's conceptual triad of space helps to understand how space is the product of relations between natural and social objects. In Lefebvre's view, the main protagonists in the production of space are urban specialists (urban planners and real-estate developers) and ordinary citizens. Through the urban spaces, movements have the potential to sustain the political change to the state. In better words, the revolutionary situations and social movements can challenge the potential dynamics and alternatives of the urban spaces. But, how do the cities reflect, work against, or attempt to contain political conflict?

One particular activity that has an enormous impact on the production of urban space is violence. Inspired by the spatial turn of scholarship on violence and public space that stems from the various forms of space production in and beyond urban (Tullumello and Pavoni 2021) and the urban conflict that emerges in response to the state violence and the interaction between state-sanctioned and the "bottom-up" forms of violence (Handel 2021), this chapter focuses on the case of the protest squares and insurgent urbanism during the political revolutions, movements, and social unrests. Focusing on analytical and methodological points of view, this chapter creates an intellectual framework for further research on radical urbanism and the production of space rather than attempting to formulate a coherent theory. Here, the main aim is to conceptualize the public space's politically productive and epidemic

DOI: 10.4324/9781003140795-5

Radical Urbanism 77

potential through the political revolutions, conflicts, movements, and social unrests.

Through developing the theoretical frameworks, the chapter aims to understand why protest squares are specific political spaces and how it relates (advertently or/and inadvertently) with the processes of political revolution, violence, and social conflict. The spatial nature of protest squares and their transformative power to transcend socio-structural constraints during the political movements raise an important inquiry: which kind of urban space was created during the political revolutions that represented the square as the symbolic place of protest and bottom-up response to state violence? Following Turner's definition of liminality, the first section of the article, "Liminality, Revolutions, and Protest Squares," aims to conceptualize the political revolutions as the liminal phenomena to analyze the transformative power of protest squares as the urban political spaces. Consequently, the second part of the research, the "Empty Place of Power," focuses on Lefort's works to conceptualize the relationship between politics, democracy, and urban space. Finally, building on Deleuze and Guattari's definition of rhizomatic democracy, this chapter introduces the features of the open (or emerging) society through protest squares, violence, and insurgent urbanism.

Building on the theoretical framework and through the historical and discourse analysis of the urban processes, the case study part of this chapter focuses on the contemporary case studies of protest square, especially in the Middle Eastern context, to contribute to a better understanding of power relations in the protest squares and socio-political contexts.

Liminality, Revolutions, and Protest Squares

The insurgent spaces like protest squares shape and define the transformative experience of revolutions as liminal spaces. In 1978, *Victor Turner* and his wife, *Edith Turner*, published *Image and Pilgrimage in Christian Culture*. Turner argued that some social processes—including revolutions and political movements—have similar *liminal* stages in which the structures of everyday life of the immediate past have been overturned. Still, new structures and systems have not yet emerged to replace them. He used the term *AntiStructure* in which most of the characteristics that defined the normal configuration of socio-political life ceased to function (Turner and Turner 1978).

Liminality (from the Latin word "līmen," meaning "a threshold") refers to the psychological effect that begins to be produced. Liminal is the adjective used to describe things associated with that point or threshold, as it is also called. Turner (1969) used *Communitas* as an intense feeling of community, solidarity, and togetherness experienced by those who live together in an *Antistructure*. The typical social statuses and positions have broken down. Yang (2000) proposes social movements as "liminal phenomena that separate participants from pre-existing structural constraints and give them the freedom and power to remold themselves and society" since movements separate their participants from existing social structures and relocate them in a liminal situation. He added, "For those involved, the total effect is a threshold effect-the experience becomes a dividing line in personal histories with immediate and long-term consequences" (380).

Victor William Turner's definition of *limen*, "threshold," is central to unfolding the relationship between *Revolutions* and *Liminality* (Bigger 2009). Places "In-Between" or "Inside-Out" Spaces are other expressions to describe "liminal" spaces. During the revolutions, squares become liminal or *inside-out* spaces where the state attempts to maintain some form of control and the public attempts to occupy it (Mehan 2020a). Liminality can refer to society in a state of revolution as one expected end, but a new, stable normal has not yet emerged.

In her book *On Revolution*, Hannah Arendt (2006) argues that modern revolutions, with their intense collective violence and destructive capacity, faced the challenge of finding a government that puts the law above man. Arendt argues that revolutions essentially foster the revolutionary spirit that energizes the masses, pursuing a pluralistic political deliberation and governance system. She argues that establishing a revolutionary inspired form of government is the primary means through which a good society is attained (5). Therefore, in a large-scale setting, political revolutions as the quintessential outbreaks of liminal conditions are entailing genuine collapse of order and loss of stable reference points (Horvath, Bjørn and Harald 2015, 6).

Harald Wylda's chapter in *Breaking Boundaries* conceives democracy as being in dialogue with a condition in which the place of power is empty. In this permanent authority vacuum, modern democracy has developed bounded spaces that challenge the political realization of freedom. According to Wydra (2005), the constitution of power in a revolution means not the limitation but the foundation and correct distribution of power (4). The liminal occurrences of revolution combine the two-objective character of a sudden event and the subjective perspective of how this event lived through by the individuals changing (Wydra 2005, 8). Yang (2000) argues that the transformative power of social movements depends on their degree of liminality. Participants' experience getting to the insurgent squares reflected a "liminal" state (Peterson 2015, 5–6). In better words, the liminal protest square and the transformative experience of revolutions are interrelated. Focusing on *Victor Turner's* notion of "processual" ritual analysis, the liminal is the second phase of a three-stage ritual process. The first stage, separation, separates the ritual subject from the previous structural condition (Turner 1969, 166–167). The second stage, the liminal, is anti-structural, where few or none of the past attributes have been left (ibid, 94). The final step is settling back into a new social structure. In better words, the liminal stage involves one or all three separations: spatial, temporal, and social/moral. When ritual subjects are separated from the familiar space, the routine temporal order, or the structures of moral obligations and social ties, they enter a liminal time/space (ibid, 41). Conceptualizing political revolutions as liminal phenomena helps explain the transformative power of protest squares. In its break with existing social structures, a socio-political movement allows its participants to transcend social structural constraints. Peterson (2015) represented the *liminal* nature of space by reintroducing the example of Tahrir Square as the symbolic place of protest in Egypt so that public demonstrations in other parts all become part of the "spirit of Tahrir" and "Freedom." In better words, occupying the square and taking the square movements around the world highlighted the global demand for participatory democracy; as a process of collective decision-making that people have the power to decide on policy. The degree of citizens' involvement can directly affect policy.

Can we theorize the formation of "democratic urban space"? What are the aspects that shape the relationship between politics and urban space? The next section of the draft reframes and analyzes the concept of *Democratic Space* through the theory of *Empty Place of Power*.

The "Empty Place of Power"

The "empty place of power" or void is one of the central theses in *Lefort's* work: the idea that political regimes are distinguished by how the place of power is represented within them. The "power" in the place of power comes from the knowledge of society as a whole that its occupant gains. It is often based on such claims to possess such knowledge that the occupant of the place of power is granted the authority to make laws. Lefort writes that the essence of power is "to present and make visible a model of social organization." In a democracy—as a political regime distinct from absolute monarchy and totalitarianism—the place of power is symbolically empty. By holding the blank as the "symbolic place of power," modern democracy can legitimate social conflict (Mehan 2017). Lefort (1988) characterizes the political (*le politique*) as "the principles that generate different forms of society." He introduces a frame that informs the political experiences of members within society (217–218). Therefore, "The Place of Power" is "organized as one despite (or because of) its multiple divisions, and it is organized as the same in all its multiple dimensions implies a reference to a place from which it can be seen, read, and named" (ibid, 225). In this sense, the existence of such a place in the symbolic order is a precondition for the experience of political society as a meaningful whole. According to *Lefort*, the birth of modern democracy is seen in the dramatic context of the downfall of absolute monarchy, the revolutionary conflict of antagonistic forces, and its associated emptiness of the place of power. Lefort stated that the emergence of the democratic form of society resulted from a series of transformations, which began to take place in medieval and early modern Europe. For Lefort (1986), the legitimacy of political power is linked to the image of an empty place (*lieu vide*), impossible to occupy, such that those who exercise public authority can never claim to appropriate it. Therefore, power appears as an empty place. Those who wield it as mere mortals who occupy it only temporarily or could install themselves in it only by force or cunning (300–305).

The modern conception of representative democracy introduces the symbol of people in two meanings, both as legitimizing the government and as participants (Voegelin 1987, 38–41). In other words, people are the source of power in a democracy, but it is the power of nobody. According to *Flynn* (2005), *Lefort's* work has set for itself the task of interpreting the political life of modern society. Flynn (2005) writes Lefort's political theory is born from a reflection on political experience and a consideration of the forms of political life (xviii–xix). The conception of totalitarianism and democracy is discussed well in *Lefort's* works. As *Flynn* clarified, "the king incarnated society's identity in the pre-modern ancient regimes. However, modernity represented 'the disincarnating of society.'" In other words, no figure can embody society's unity. What is important here is that in a modern democracy, the king occupied remains *empty*. This openness or non-identity is a prerequisite by a modern democracy. However, totalitarianism as a "counterrevolution against democracy" is a response that tries to fill the "empty place of power" with a materialization of "the people-as-one" (Dallmayr 2006). Revolutionary experiences create new meanings as they reverse taken-for-granted meanings, thus achieving contradictory meanings of symbols. In this sense, the emergence of democracy followed through a typology of spatial experiences in the empty place of power, where the situational premises reconfigure political symbolism (Wydra 2005, 26). But is it possible to achieve real democracy through protest squares? Which definition of democracy can represent the transformative feature of global urban social movements? The next part introduces the concept of *Rhizomatic* Democracy to redefine the features of emerging society through recent social movements.

Urban Social Movements as "Rhizomatic" Democracy

In 1964, *Henri Lefebvre* (2009), in a short piece entitled *Les Sources de la théorie marxiste-lenininste de l 'etat'* writes:

> Democracy is nothing other than the struggle for democracy. The struggle for democracy is the movement itself. Many democrats imagine that democracy is a type of stable condition toward which can tend, toward which we must tend. Democracy is the movement. Moreover, the movement is the forces in action. In addition, democracy is the struggle for democracy, which is to say the very movement of social forces; it is a permanent struggle and it is even a struggle against the state that emerges from democracy. There is no democracy without a struggle against the democratic state itself, which tends to consolidate itself as a block, to affirm itself as a whole, become monolithic and to smother the society out of which develops.
>
> (61)

The book *What is Philosophy?* by *Gilles Deleuze* and *Félix Guattari* asks whether philosophy in its critical form is closely aligned with "the modern democratic state and human rights." They point out that there is no universal democratic state since the market is the only thing under universal capitalism (Deleuze and Guattari 1987, 102–104). Deleuze and Guattari's adherence to a Nietzschean image of thought as creation leads them to advocate a "utopian" conception of philosophy, which provides the key to their relationship to democracy. For *Deleuze* and *Guattari*, democracy is a *rhizomatic* politics rather than a politics of demonstration. It is a politics situated in the middle of all senses, horizontally, between equals, with equal and unprivileged capacities for opinion and choice, and vertically, under the absence of transcendent values (Mengue 2003). In a broader sense, *Deleuzian* political philosophy criticizes the present democracy and searches for "the contour, the configuration, and the constellation of an event to come" (Deleuze and Guattari 1994, 32–33).

In other words, democracy is a process of becoming instead of a state of being. Therefore, instead of *being democratic, becoming democratic* will be the main issue. But which kind of urban society is needed to become democratic? For describing the particular characteristics of democratic urban society, *Lefebvre*, in his book *Urban Revolution* clarified that it is ruled by urban inhabitants who appropriate space and claim it as their own to meet their needs (Purcell 2013).

In 1970, Henri Lefebvre, in his book *Urban Revolution* distinguished between the two different notions of the industrial city and urban society. According to Purcell, by the industrial city, Lefebvre means the Capitalist city, as he inhabited it in 1970, a city in which the dominant socio-spatial processes separate and segregate people from another. In this sense, urban inhabitants of the industrial city are politically passive, and they function primarily as consumers rather than citizens (Purcell 2013).

Further definitions of the characteristics of urban society represent it as ongoing urban practice in the process of formation. In the introduction of A New Philosophy of Society (2006), Manuel De Landa refers to "the relatively few pages dedicated to assemblage theory in the work of Deleuze" and explains how he deals with this difficulty. De Landa (2006) suggests that it is not only a paucity of words that is a problem for his study, but also the way the definition, extension, and qualification of the concept of assemblage is dispersed throughout Deleuze's works. He enumerates the strategies he proposes to engage in Deleuzian hermeneutics: "I will give my own definitions of the technical terms, use my own argument to justify them, and use entirely different theoretical resources to develop them" (3).

Based on *Lefebvre's* (2003) writings, "urban society can be defined not as an accomplished reality...but, on the contrary, like a horizon, illuminating virtually. Therefore, it can be defined as an ongoing social practice, an urban practice in the process of formation.... this practice is currently veiled and disjointed...it possesses only fragments of reality and a science that is still in the future. Our job is to demonstrate that such an approach has an outcome, that there are solutions to the current problem" (16–17). Similarly, *Deleuze* (1966), in his book *Le Bergsonisme*, presented the community in the process of becoming as never stable, always open to the future, always resisting the forces that repress and impede "the whole of freedom" (112). Deleuzian's definition of "open society," suggests a "society of creators" who gain access to "the open creative totality" through acting and creating (ibid, 117–118).

Henri Lefebvre (2003) in his book *The Urban Revolution* argues that "The passivity of those involved, their silence, and their reticent prudence are an indication of the absence of urban democracy, that is, concrete democracy. Urban revolution and concrete (developed) democracy coincide." In this sense, people are autonomous rather than heteronomous, *meaning literally that people* "give themselves the law" rather than having the "law given to them by another" (Purcell 2013, 314).

Focusing on the notion of community, Kozlowski, Mehan and Nawratek (2020), in the book *"Kuala Lumpur: Community, Infrastructure, and Urban Inclusivity,"* defined the community as "an empty signifier that allows different elements to associate in a relation of equivalence and represents an antagonistic boundary defining their limits such as excluding the fundamentally different 'other.'" Following the empty signifier theoretical framework, community is defined as the discursive element that has been emptied of its actual content and provides for the unity of the discourse (Kozlowski, Mehan and Nawratek 2020, 28). Therefore, the entities, networks, and structures can also be imposed by special actors that have primarily been established by political acts of hegemonic closure (Mehan et al. 2022a).

In a broader perspective, if we consider the goal of revolutionary becoming of the people is to *resist the present* (Deleuze and Guattari 1994, 107–108), is there a link between "becoming democratic" and "becoming revolutionary"? We can argue that "becoming revolutionary" is a prerequisite of "becoming democratic." For *Deleuze* and *Guattari*, revolutionary becoming aims at "the intensive, untimely, not a moment but a becoming," which is always underway (ibid, 112). In *Deleuze* and *Guattari's* term, democracy can be defined by "the people to come" who are "missing or lacking in the actual world" who "have a chance to invent themselves" by resisting what is intolerable in the present (ibid, 110). So, to achieve a "new community whose members are capable of a belief in themselves, in the world and in becoming," we need both "creativity" and "the people" (Deleuze 1995, 176). This new community is defined based on what *Deleuze* and *Guattari* (1994) call a "revolutionary and liberation utopia," which imposes a new blueprint of norms and laws (100). In experimenting with such revolutionary groups whose members engage in horizontal, non-hierarchical relations, *Deleuze* and *Guattari* use the imagery of rhizomes: center-less assemblages in which any point or individual can connect to any other. The idea of a body (politics) without organs (party) is the central debate in what Deleuze and Guattari are proposing (Purcell 2013). Such organ-less bodies are all made up of a multitude of individuals that can act quite effectively as a mass without any centralized leadership. So, can we refer to protest squares as the struggles to move toward Lefebvre's concept of urban society?

In 1972, In his book *Invisible Cities* (Italian: *Le città invisibili*), Italo Calvino depicted imaginary conversations between the Venetian explorer Marco Polo and the aged Mongol ruler Kulabi Khan which can be instrumental in framing approaches to urban discourse and the form of the city. Calvino (1972) presented the concept of *the inferno* as follows: "The inferno of the living is not something that will be; if there is one, it is what is already here, the inferno where we live every day that we form by being together. There are two ways to escape suffering. The first is easy for many: accept the inferno and become such a part of it that you can no longer see it. The second is risky and demands constant vigilance and apprehension: seek and learn to recognize who and what, amid inferno, are not inferno, then make them endure, give them space" (164). In other words, the emerging elements of urban society amid *inferno* need space to be recognized. So, can the urban social movements help people reclaim and develop their power? Focusing on *Italo Calvino*'s phrase "give it space," occupy movements could be represented as the physical space for smoothing the path toward fulfilling the democratic urban society. This emerging society is not a socialist utopia, but rather a possible society that is rudimentary and in the process of becoming.

Squares as Politics

The recent examples of protest square worldwide highlighted the formation of political space through protest squares (Figure 4.1). The recent Euromaidan protest in Ukraine presents an interesting case: a grassroots movement sparked in the fall of 2013 by a relatively small group of protesters turned into a much broader and larger mass protest against government corruption and for human rights and dignity. Before Ukraine's Euromaidan drew the world's attention in 2013, there were only a handful of recent studies looking at countries such as Georgia, Ukraine, and other former Soviet republics where "revolutions" of sorts have occurred (Rose Revolution in Georgia in 2003, Orange Revolution in Ukraine in 2004, among others) (Lokot 2021, 6).

The contemporary case studies of protest square, especially in the Middle Eastern context, can contribute to a better understanding of power relations and ideological symbolism through social formation

Radical Urbanism 85

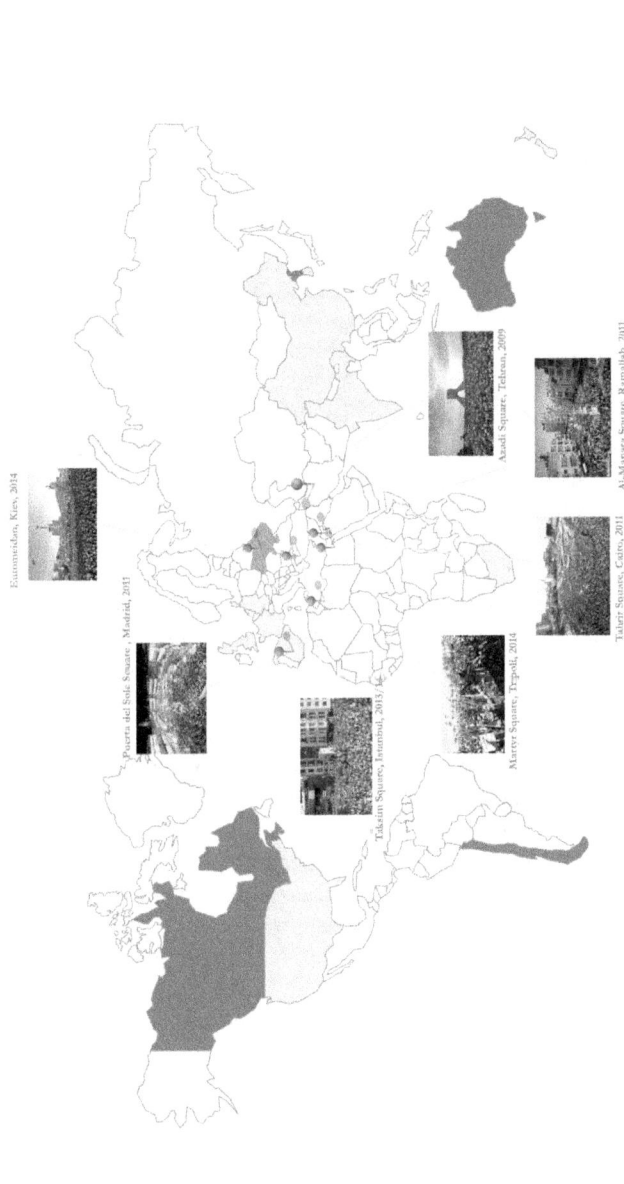

Figure 4.1 Tahrir Square (Cairo, 2011), Azadi Square (Tehran, 2009), Taksim Square (Istanbul, 2013–2014), Syntagma Square (Athens, 2010/2012), Puerta del Sol Square (Madrid, 2011–present), Euromaidan or maidan Nezalezhnosti literally means independent Square (Kiev, 2013/14), Palaza de la Catalunya (Barcelona, 2011), Paternoster Square (London, 2011), Martyr's Square or *Maydān ash-Shuhadā*, Previously Saha el khadra Green Square (Tripoli, 2011), Al-Manara Square (Ramallah, 2011), and Pearl Roundabout or Lu'u Roundabout (Bahrein, 2011) are some protest squares after 2000.

Source: Author.

86 *Radical Urbanism*

processes. In the Middle East, protests have been more antagonistic to the State's power and institutions. Accordingly, they have been more spontaneous, conflictual, and influential in threatening the power structures and the political establishment and changing the hegemonic cityscapes (Zamani and Mehan 2019, 483). The centrality of insurgent squares in the recent social protests worldwide highlighted the crucial role of physical urban spaces as essential arenas for staging protests and political actions. The insurgent urbanism produced during the global occupy movement and many protests sweeping through the Middle-East suggests that the public square has become a proverbial "center stage" that holds a symbolically meaningful collective memory (Mehan 2020b, 64–65).

In Tehran, the recent movements highlighted the socio-political importance of Shahyad (renamed to Azadi/Freedom) Square and Revolution (in Farsi Enqelab) Street as spaces of Protests and political conflict. The Shahyad (literally means In the Memory of King) monument was built in 1971 on the western edge of Tehran (near the Mehrabad airport) on the 2,500th anniversary of founding the Persian Empire by the Great Cyrus. On December 12, 1978, Shahyad Square, a brand-new showcase square in the western part of Tehran, provided an open space for revolutionaries. More than two million people occupied the Square in protest against Mohammad Reza Shah Pahlavi. The Square became available to everybody, and the crowd was claiming a revolution out of the Square's public space. As a Shah's (previous king) icon in the heart of Tehran, rather than being destroyed, it continues to be a focal point for national celebrations, political protests, massive demonstrations, and social movements (Figure 4.2).

Many public spaces throughout Tehran experienced re-identification after the Islamic Revolution. Like many other public spaces in Post-revolutionary Iran, the Shahyad square "earned" its new name— *Azadi* or Freedom Square—through its role as an important gathering place for protesters throughout the movement that eventually overthrew the Shah of Iran. *Azadi* Square became the most recognizable icon that people around the world now associate with the Islamic Revolution of 1979. Since the revolution of 2011, the revolutionalized notion of the "Tahrir effect" remains evident in what a public space is about (Abaza 2014). Like *Tahrir*, the mere mention of *Azadi* Square in Tehran evokes memories of people in the iconic physical square who have the power to confront an autocratic political system.

The urban centers of the uprisings, such as *Azadi* Square and *Enqelab* Square in Tehran, became symbolic nodes of struggles between citizens and state power. The above-mentioned urban

Radical Urbanism 87

Figure 4.2 Azadi Square in Tehran.
Source: Atlas de Téhéran métropole, Vol. 1. La terre et les homes (2005).

spaces in Tehran hold a spatial significance as sites of protest and urban mobilization that evoke the collective political memory of the 1979 revolution since they were actively contesting the meaning and memory of the previous revolution (Mehan 2020b). These insurgent geographic locations had played a significant symbolic role during the Islamic Revolution of 1978–1979 and, as such, endowed with euphoric and historical meanings, as the birthplace of the Islamic Revolution. The Iranian presidential election of 2009 has been compared to the demonstrations leading up to the 1979 Islamic Revolution. Almost three decades later, the new generation of Iranians flooded the Azadi square to protest against the revolutionary regime, which has become an entrenched theocratic autocracy. It is important to note that the historical importance of protest squares and the collective memory of the past revolutions matters. The case of Azadi Square as a prestigious project by the shah that became an anti-project after the Islamic Revolution shows the significance of this relationship and, more, in particular, clarifies the capacity of this square—as the national symbol of Iran endowed with euphoric and historical meaning—to host both pro- and anti-government demonstrations.

In post-revolutionary Iran and starting from 2017 and continuing into 2018, the new wave of women's protests in Iran was initially inspired by an Iranian woman known for standing in protest on a utility box in the Enqelab (Revolution Street) in Tehran on December 28, 2017. The young protesters—known as "daughters of the revolution"—tied their white scarves (hijab) to the sticks and waved them in protest. After this act of insubordination, the women re-enacted her march (and posted photos of their actions), being branded as the "Girls of Revolution Street" on social media (Mehan & Rossi, 2019, 239–240). After the recent protest in Tehran, in June 2018, the city council passed a bill to depoliticize and demarcate certain places (12 locations or protest zones) for demonstrations and political expression. Normalizing protest and re-appropriating the specific appropriate locations of public protests shows the emerging forms of control and domination by the state-led authorities over the protest squares and the public spaces.

Major Findings

Suppose we consider the urban society and democracy as elements that are struggling to emerge. The protest squares and then take the square movements can be defined as the systemic response to the deep economic and political crisis. As discussed before, the liminal feature of protest squares during the political revolutions as the spaces where the state attempts to maintain some form of control and where the public tries to occupy opens up a new perspective. In these liminal spaces, one expected end, but a new, stable normal has not emerged yet. As a result, protest squares can shape and define the transformative experience of revolutions as liminal spaces. As discussed previously, the case of Freedom Square in Tehran as a prestigious project by shah that became an anti-project after the Islamic Revolution proves this claim. Rather than being destroyed, it continues to be a gathering point to host pro- and anti-government demonstrations, social movements, conflicts, and political protests.

Using the theoretical notions of liminality, the empty place of power and rhizomatic democracy enable us to analyze how squares—as the political objects—are partly shaped by the logic of violence (Mehan 2020c). Using Turner's three-stage ritual process (*antistructure, liminal,* and *communitas*) in protest squares helps theorize the transformative processes of insurgent urbanism during the political revolutions and social movements. In the first place, protest squares became *antistructure* (in Turner's term), in which most of the characteristics that defined the *normal* configuration of socio-political life ceased to function. In the second step, the *liminal* is where few or none of the past attributes have been left. The final stage, *Communitas,* is settling back into a new social structure with an intense feeling of community and solidarity experienced by those who broke down the social statuses and resisted violence. This epidemic sense of solidarity heralds the protest squares' political message to inspire other movements worldwide.

The experiences of the recent occupy movements and protest squares worldwide stress the global demand for participatory democracy to legitimate the social conflict. To conceptualize and imagine the space of participatory democracy, which introduces the people as both legitimizing the government and being represented, we need to create "an empty place of power." In other words, in this democratic space, people are sources of power, but it is the power of nobody so that no figure can embody the society's unity (Mehan et al. 2022b). This openness or non-identical feature of "empty place of power," is the same feature in protest squares during the social movements and political revolutions. So, democracies should have empty centers (like protest squares to contain the conflict). For fulfilling the idea of "becoming" democrat (instead of "being" democrat), Lefebvrian "urban society" or Deleuzian "open society" is never stable, always open to the future, always resisting the forces, and violence that repress and impede "the whole of freedom." This definition of unstable "open society" in "Rhizomatic Politics" connected the processes of "becoming democratic" and "becoming revolutionary," which is always underway. To resist what is intolerable in the present and achieve an open society, we need the "people to come" who "have the chance to invent themselves."

References

Abaza, Mona. 2014. "Post January Revolution Cairo: Urban Wars and the Reshaping of Public Space." *Theory, Culture and Society* 31 (7–8): 163–183.
Arendt, Hannah. 2006. *On Revolution*. New York: Penguin.
Bigger, Stephen. 2009. "Victor Turner, Liminality, and Cultural Performance." *Journal of Beliefs & Values* 30 (2): 209–212.
Calvino, Italo. 1972. *Le Citta Invisibili*. Verona: Mondadori.
Dallmayr, Fred. 2006. "The Philosophy of Claude Lefort: Interpreting the Political." *Notre Dame Philosophical Reviews*. Paris: University of Notre Dame.
De Landa, Manuel. 2006. *A New Philosophy of Society: Assemblage Theory and Social Complexity*. New York: Continuum.
Deleuze, Gilles, and Félix Guattari. 1987. *A Thousand Plateaus*. Translated by B Massumi. Minneapolis: University of Minnesota Press.
—. 1994. *What Is Philosophy?* Translated by H. Tomlinson and G. Burchell, 107–108. New York: Columbia University Press.
Deleuze, Gilles. 1966. *Le Bergsonisme*. Paris: Presses universitaries de France.
—. 1995. *Negotiations*. Translated by Martin Joughin. New York: Colombia University Press.
Flynn, Bernard. 2005. *The Philosophy of Claude Lefort: Interpreting the Political*. Evanston, Illinois: Northwestern University Press.
Handel, Ariel. 2021. "Urban Violence: the Dialectics of City-Making and Ruination in Settler-Colonial Settings." *Lo Squaderno: Explorations in Space and Society* (59).
Horvath, Agnes, Thomassen Bjørn, and Wydra Harald. 2015. *Breaking Boundaries: Varieties of Liminality*. Oxford, New York: Berghahn Books.
Kozlowski, Marek, Asma Mehan, and Krzysztof Nawratek. 2020. "Kuala Lumpur: Community, Infrastructure and Urban Inclusivity", in *The Built Environment City Studies- Focus Series*, 1st edition: 142. London: Routledge, Taylor and Francis Group.
Lefebvre, Henri. 1991. *The Production of Space*, Translated by Donald Nicholson-Smith. London: Wiley-Blackwell Publishers.
—. 2003. *The Urban Revolutions*. Minnesota: University of Minnesota Press.
—. 2009. *State, Space, World: Selected Essays*. Minneapolis: University of Minnesota Press.
Lefort, Claude. 1986. *The Political Forms of Modern Society: Bureaucracy, Democracy, Totalitarianism*, 300–305. Cambridge: MIT Press.
—. 1988. *Democracy and Political Theory*, Translated by David Macey, 217–218. Cambridge: Polity Press.
Lokot, Tetyana. 2021. *Beyond the Protest Square: Digital Media and Augmented Dissent*. London; New York: Rowman & Littlefield International.
Mehan, Asma, Carolina Lima, Faith Ng'eno, and Krzysztof Nawratek. 2022a. "Questioning Hegemony Within White Academia." *Field* 8 (1): 47–61.
Mehan, Asma, Bouchra Tafrata, Vladan Klement, and Salma Tabi. 2022b. "A Radical Manifesto", In *Manifesto for the Just City*, by Roberto Rocco and Caroline Newton, 64–67. Delft, the Netherlands: TU Delft Open.

Mehan, Asma. 2017. "Review of 'The Empty Place: Democracy and Public Space' by Teresa Hoskyns." *ID: International Dialogue, A Multidisciplinary Journal of World Affairs* 7: 86–90.
—. 2020a. "The City as the (Anti) Structure: Fearscapes, Social Movement, and Protest Square." *Lo Squaderno: Explorations in Space and Society* (57).
—. 2020b. "Emerging 'spatialities of discontent' in Modern Tehran", In *Iranian Cities. An Emerging Agenda at a Time of Drastic Alterations*, by Coppola Alessandro and Fadaei Arman, 63–71. Macerata: Quodlibet.
—. 2020c. "The Destructive Characther". In *Vademecum: 77 Minor Terms for Writing Urban Places*, by K. Havik, K. Pint, S. Riesto and H. Steiner, 62–63. Rotterdam: nai0I0publishers.
Mehan, Asma and Rossi Ugo. 2019. "Multiplying Resistance: the Power of the Urban in the Age of National Revanchism", in *Philosophy and the City: Interdisciplinary and Transcultural Perspectives*, by Malpas Jeff, Jacobs Kate, 233–245. London: Rowman & Littlefield International.
Mengue, Philippe. 2003. *Deleuze Et La Question De La Démocratie*. Paris: L'Harmattan.
Peterson, Mark Allen. 2015. "In Search of Antistructure: The Meaning of Tahrir Square in Egypt's Ongoing Social Drama", in *Breaking Boundaries: Varieties of Liminality*, by Horvath Agnese, Wydra Harald, and Thomassen Bjørn, 5–6. New York: Berghahn Books.
Purcell, Mark. 2013. "Possible Worlds: Henri Lefebvre and the Right to the City." *Journal of Urban Affairs* 36: 141–154.
—. 2013. "The Right to the City: the Struggle for Democracy in the Urban Public Realm." *Policy and Politics* 43 (3): 311–327.
Tullumello, Simone, and Andrea Pavoni. 2021. "Editorial: Beyond Urban Violence." *Lo Squaderno – Explorations in Space and Society* 59: 6–7.
Turner, Victor, and Edith Turner. 1978. *Image and Pilgrimage in Christian Culture*. New York: Columbia University Press.
Turner, Victor. 1969. "Liminality and Communitas", in *The Ritual Process: Structure and Anti-Structure*. Chicago: Aldine Publishing.
Voegelin, Eric. 1987. *The New Science of Politics: An Introduction*, 38–41. Chicago: University of Chicago Press.
Wydra, Harald. 2005. "Approaching the Empty Space of Power: Revolutions and Political Order, Faculty of Political Science and Sociology", University of Granada, ECPR Joint Sessions.
Yang, Guobin. 2000. "The Liminal Effects of Social Movements: Red Guards and the Transformation of Identity." *Sociological Forum* 15 (3): 379–406.
Zamani, Farzad, and Asma Mehan. 2019. "The Abstract Space and the Alienation of Political Public Space in the Middle East." *Archnet-IJAR: International Journal of Architectural Research* 13 (3): 483–497.

5 Insurgent Cities

Protest Democracy

Environmental challenges, forced immigration, class struggle, radical exclusion, pandemic outbreak, and economic inequalities deepen the democracy crisis across the globe (Mehan and Tafrata 2022). As Jeffery Hou (2020) highlights: "unsanctioned, unscripted, and seemingly undesirable activities have long appropriated urban spaces in routine and sometimes unexpected ways, bringing new meaning and unforeseen functions to those spaces. They occupy or appropriate urban spaces in routine and sometimes unexpected ways, bringing new meanings and unforeseen functions to those places. In many cities worldwide, these activities are an integral part of the quotidian urban landscapes and systems of everyday life. Together, they encompass short-term, temporary actions and ongoing struggles and contestations" (Hou 2020, 117).

The success of cities must supplement states' efforts in order to increase sovereign incapacities without pretending nations away or making them villains in the story of democratic globalization (Barber 2013, 11). As Frug and Barron (2008) emphasized: "Cities are schoolhouses of democracy, and can retain their ability to enable people to learn the skills of self-government only if they are given sufficient power to make decisions and have tangible consequences for the quality of local life" (50). The Greeks gave the name polis to their early communities, which was a politicized collection of tribes (so-called demes) in the case of archetypical Athens. As Aristotle once called the man a political animal (a zoon politikon), Edward Glaeser (2011) today speaks of humankind as an "urban species," whose cities are "made of flesh, not concrete" (15). To consider the city's future as a foundation for democratic global governance, also means looking to the city's past and its ancient democratic origins (Barber 2013, 14).

DOI: 10.4324/9781003140795-6

Insurgent Cities 93

However, based on Saskia Sassen's (2001) suggestions: "what contributes to growth in the network of global cities may well not contribute to growth in nations" (9). The Occupy Movement of 2011 provides an example of the new wave of social unrest and protest movements. Occupy emerged in a period of crisis for liberal democracy. One of the most visible signs of this crisis is the widespread disengagement of the citizenry from institutional political processes in developed countries (Taylor 2017, 2–3). The increasing disaffection of youth with liberal politics, voting, the rise of consumer culture, and the explosion of social media, such as Facebook, Instagram, and Twitter, can be seen as intensifying the alienation that operates under a market capitalist ethos rather than a democratic one (Taylor 2017, 4).

The recent Black Lives Matter movement using hashtag #BLM has reignited decentralized transnational political and social campaigns to fight racism, discrimination, and inequality. The Grassroots reactions and protests to colonial remnants in the urban landscape were as important. The social protests and social movements to colonial remnants in the urban landscape raise a new critical voice and public awareness. Back to March 2015, in Cape Town, the campaign "Rhodes must fall," for example, demanded the statue of British imperialist Cecil Rhodes be removed. This campaign received international attention and led to a broader movement to "decolonize" history, education, and material culture worldwide.

Similarly, in Bristol, the bronze statue of Edward Colston was thrown in the water by protestors. These "Statues must fall" campaigns and protestors also affect the public spaces and urban squares. London Mayor—Sadiq Khan—for instance announced a new commission to review the capital's urban landmarks. Contradictorily, more conservative voices and governments have spoken out against these protests. For instance, President Trump issued an executive order protecting "American monuments and memorial statues" in the United States. (Mehan, Sennema and Tideman 2020). The leaderless and unaffiliated "Gilet-Jaunes" uprisings, known as the longest-running protest in France since the Second World War, began with ordinary people who refused to accept the new eco fuel taxes. The protests took place in cities and small towns and on almost every local square and roundabout by refusing to be bound with the agreed protest venues, routes, and marshals. In refusing to accept an ecological transition designed by technocratic patricians and paid for by the precariat, the "Gilet Jaunes" has inaugurated what Swyngedouw (2018) would recognize as a process of depoliticization; a process in which "fundamentally political questions [are asked about] who gains from and who pays for, who benefits from and who suffers (and in what ways) from particular processes of metabolic, circulatory change" (89). Thus, it is in Gezi and Zuccotti Park; Syntagma Square, Taksim, and Azadi Square, from Tehran and Istanbul to Hong Kong and New York; that processes of politicization are inaugurated as bodies come together in public space to declare a wrong and stage their equality.

Cosmopolitanism responds by imagining citizens rooted in urban neighborhoods reaching to confront the central power where participation, solidarity, and community are still possible, calling across frontiers to confront and contain central authority. By expanding and diversifying the citizens' cooperation networks, cities prove they can do things together that states cannot (Barber 2013, 5–6). Social movements are essential drivers of social change in the fight to overcome the crisis of democracy (Marx and Engels 2012, 49). As Jackie Smith and Dawn Wiest (2012) state: "History has shown that significant societal transformation only happens when those excluded from power and privilege confront and challenge the existing social order. Moreover, in times of crisis, elites are most vulnerable to pressures from social movements, and more radical change becomes possible." In this context, neoliberalism needs to be seen as a participatory *political* response to the democratic gains that had been previously achieved by working classes and which had become, from capital "perspective, barriers to accumulations" (Panitch and Gindin 2013, 15). In better words, protest opens possibilities for rethinking and challenging existing structures, and journalists use protest as "a liminal space of possibility" (Tenenboum-Weinblatt 2014). The next part aims to introduce the "Take the Square" movement as an example of democratic, non-hierarchical, and participatory protest platform.

Take the Square

If the city planning was concerned with furthering democratic participation, the protest squares highlighted the inherently political character of using public space in urban settings. Over the last decade, in response to globalization, there have been many protests, social movements, and some democratic assemblies like *Take the Square* and *Right to the City (RTTC)*, which have risen throughout the world (Mehan 2017). But can this growing social movement create democratic space in future cities?

Protest square as a new global phenomenon came to stand as an emerging process of revolutionary transformations from the Middle

East to Europe and the United States. *Take the Square* movement was born from the demonstration on May 15, 2011, in Madrid. The rally was called from *Democracia Real Ya* (Real Democracy Now). The idea of camping in the square as a way of demonstrating against a dominant and oppressive system, led by a political class working and as a way to promote new initiatives of political, social, economic, artistic, and cultural organization, generated the concept of "Take the Square" which was created in the camp of *Madrid (AcampadaSol)* and then exported to the rest of the cities in Spain and the world. Some of the general slogans in this new *Take the Square* movement concentrated on the Occupy Strategies and the ways to achieve real democracy. In a map below, some of the "Take the square network" has been shown, which has been spread mostly in Europe (Greece, Italy, France, Spain, UK, Belgium, Portugal, and Netherland), some states of the US (New York, San Francisco, and Wisconsin), Latin America (Buenos Aires and Brazil) and Auckland. With popular slogans like *how to occupy* and *Yes We Camp*, this social movement tries to establish an international network of citizen activism based on the protest squares ideals. Thus, the 15M movements in Spain, with its slogan *Real Democracia Ya* (Real Democracy Now), drew the bright and inspiring line that all popular protest movements would follow. But is there any influential urban social movement on a global scale? To answer this question, the next part will be focused on the Global Municipalism Movement also known as the Fearless Cities/Cities of Change.

Fearless Cities: The Global Municipalism Movement

Fearless Cities, also known as Cities of Change, Indy Towns, Communalism, and Municipalism, is an informal global movement of activists, organizations, councilors, and mayors that are working to radicalize democracy, build the participatory power structure, provide alternatives to far-right, feminize politics, and drive the transition to an economy that cares for people and our environment. The first Fearless Cities event in June 2017 turned Barcelona into an international meeting point with more than 700 people representing over 100 municipal organizations from every continent. The book documenting the first Fearless city Summit has been translated into five languages. Since then, decentralized, regional Fearless Cities events have been organized in Brussels, Valparaiso, New York City, Warsaw, Belgrade, and Naples by local municipalism platforms.[1]

Through providing the policy toolkit in various urban agendas such as the housing, public space, and local economies, the municipalism movement involves questioning the patriarchal models of organization and power and putting care in the heart of its modes of organization. In this sense, the notion of liberation municipalism is defined as the third way out of the deadlock between the capitalist or socialist models, with the faceless bureaucracies that are never responsive to the people. By inspiring from the direct democratic politics and citizen self-governance, municipal politics aims to bring forward a progressive agenda based on decentralized democracy in which ordinary people act together to chart a rational future without the need for the centralized state bureaucracy (Bookchin 2019, 15). Giving power to the ordinary people in a social justice agenda and building resilient communities mean to take the politics into every corner of the neighborhoods at the local level to foster sharing, participation, co-production, care, mutual aid, micro-networks, and solidarity (Mehan and Mostafavi 2022). For instance, the Amsterdam and Brussels-based Common Network is a collaboratory for the social and ecological transition which seeks the new models of economy and society to bring people and ideas together to provide tools and insights for social movements, collaborative government, and community groups throughout Europe and across the world.[2] As an example of the global platform more in line with the international institutions and the broader agenda for human rights, the next section aims to analyze the Global Platform for the Right to the City (GRP2C).

The Global Platform for the Right to the City

Over the past decade, some policy circles like UN-HABITAT and UNESCO have led an effort to conceptualize the Right to the city (R2C) as part of broader agenda for human rights (Purcell 2013, 141). The early dialogues such as meetings as Eco-92 in Rio de Janeiro, the Human Settlements Conference (Habitat II) in 1996 Istanbul saw success in bringing together and introducing the R2C components into Agenda 21 and the Habitat Agenda and especially the World Social Forum and the World Urban Forum, by defining adequate living conditions that should be achieved in human settlements.

The UN Conference on Housing and Sustainable Development (Habitat III) convened in *Quito, Ecuador*-2016 after a long interval between Habitat Conferences, which took place in Vancouver in 1976, and Habitat II, called in *Istanbul* 20 years later. One issue under discussion in the New Urban Agenda was the *Right to The City*, an umbrella term articulated by the French philosopher Henri Lefebvre in the 1968 book "*Le Droit à la ville*" more than 50 years ago. The World Charter

Insurgent Cities 97

for the Right to the City defines the term as "the equitable usufruct of cities within the principles of sustainability, democracy, equity, and social justice." However, some other scholars presented Right to the City, a slogan that expresses a desire for "radical transformation in urban politics." The shared vision of R2C has been supported by more than 250 local, national, regional, and international organizations that have contributed to the platform. The GPR2C is a concept that represents a "politically useful framing for increased calls for a far more explicit and pragmatic construction of participatory spaces capable of transcending scale and building novel alliances between stakeholder groups" (Frediani and Lima 2015).

Strongly associated with urban-scale calls for social justice and social change, GPR2C has come into widespread use in academics and in politics and policy that incorporates the concepts of urban developments, equity, and power relationships. As *Edward Soja* (2010) articulated, the sociopolitical production of spatial justice is one of the general and dominant critical spatial thinking. The GPR2C advocators have emphasized two main issues have been the insistence on the importance of the use-value (as opposed to the capitalist exchange value) of urban space and resources; and the claim that the power to shape the city should belong equally to all its inhabitants (Purcell 2014). In this regard, GPR2C fuses a synthetic critique of global capitalism with a call to political mobilization framed through the language of rights. Moreover, GPR2C has been defined based on three primary pillars: the first pillar is spatially just resource distribution which envisions "a socially and spatially just distribution and planning of material resources, ensuring good living conditions across the human settlement continuum." The second pillar is the political agency which is realized "when structures, processes, and policies enable all inhabitants as social and political actors to exercise the full content and meaning of citizenship." The third pillar is socio-cultural diversity, which fully "embraces diversity and difference in gender, identity, ethnicity, religion, heritage, collective memory, cultural and economic practice, and socio-cultural expression." These urban social movements are likely to serve as a model for using the urban space for democratic performance with its successes. GPR2C is a political project that challenges a neoliberal model of governance and leads to a radically different urban society.[3]

Inspired by Lefebvre's proposals related to art activism and urban social movements, several scholars argue for conceiving the urban environment as an interactive space. It is important to note that the radical nature of the GPR2C concept in practical terms tends to depoliticize the notion (Busquet 2013). Especially in the global north, the GPR2C agenda has been taken up at broader scales—most often by international development organizations—to promote and re-legitimate the pre-existing development aims, which usually leads to losing its critical edge (Athrope and Horak 2021, 2). These contradictions on the practical formulation of the GPR2C contribute to the narrative of technology as a solution to societal problems and contemporary challenges (Caprotti 2014). Defining the GPR2C as the rights of all inhabitants to occupy, use, and produce inclusive and sustainable cities implies governments and people's responsibility to claim, defend, and promote this right.

Digital Agency and Protest Movements: Squares in the Digital Era

The digitalization of everyday activities and social interaction described above is connected to a change in the use of public space. There is an ongoing scholarly debate on the dualist and hybrid nature of networked technologies which has altered the dynamics of political communication in all kinds of states.

The scholars cast the light on how social media platforms—and other digital media—have been constitute agents in the making of social movement processes happen that sustained the mobilization in point. For instance, Kavada (2015) explains how social media plays a distinctive role in creating the collective actor behind anti-austerity and pro-democracy movements. According to Castells (2015), the presence and diffusion of social media platforms and other forms of Internet-based social networks are necessary for the existence of the new social movements in our time to organize protest (Castells 2015, 226). In a similar vein, Costanza-Chock (2012) emphasizes the relationship between activist cultures and digital technologies in the Occupy Wall Street mobilizations. The social media platforms function as effective "public megaphones" for activists who want to reach out to the general public beyond the social movement milieu (Gerbaudo 2017, 137). However, scholars have cautioned that internet and social media are not by default built to be a platform for protests, revolutions, and uprisings as there are many criteria such as the popularity of a given platform in a country and the ease of performing a required action that might influence the protest organized by social media. Bennett and Segerberg (2013) argue that social media platforms put the individualized experiences of activists at the forefront of mobilization, leaving the collectivities that constitute social movement processes in the background.

The material and the digital elements of a social protest's hybrid reality make up the protest event. In an empirical analysis of Syntagma Square protests in Athens, Alice Mattoni (2020) states: "to appreciate the manifold interactions of activists with the media in an age of media abundance; we should employ an approach to social movements' culture that can grasp the nuances of activists' shared cognitive, emotional and moral understandings and their concrete embodiments of what it takes to make a social movement occur, develop and thrive" (1768). In a similar study on the case of Taksim square protests in Turkey in 2013, Brian, Men and Al-Sinan (2015) suggest that social media users seek to influence through vicarious experience—representation of the experience of others—than direct personal experience. In a better word, they suggest that social media is used to effect change from a distance, and the content ownership and online reputation are driving forces of online participation in a protest movement (499). Thus, an innovative interdisciplinary inquiry is required to see the complicated relations of digital media's role in protest activity inspired by its geographic and political contextualization (Lokot 2021, 2–3). Studies suggest that the protest activities and the main features of the culture of participation (such as radical inclusivity, multiple narrations, and mosaic-like nature) are augmented by fusing offline and online structures and mechanisms. This hybrid multiplicity offers individuals a variety of modes of participation and makes the potentialities for collective action and participatory process accessible to a diverse range of players.

Screening Dissent: Visual Narratives of Protest Squares

The technological revolution and appropriation of internet tools began to reshape the material basis of society and the urban space in the forms of collaborative, leaderless, and participatory actions. The protest squares' representation on television screens and mainstream media has been broad. Robertson (2019) defines the term "screen" as the following: "To Italians in the *quattrocento*, the screen or *schermo* was a protection against something on the outside, and got in the way of seeing. The screen used by Anglophones in the 16th and 17th centuries was still protective (usually against fire) and could also be a partition. In the early 19th century, the screen was defined as the new phenomenon that could 'open our gaze to something hidden'" (4). Described as a "window on the world," the television screen is both

"Old" and "New" embedded in various social and political environments. In the urban square, giant screens from the backdrop to the sea of small ones in what Casetti (2013) refers to as a "screen explosion." As a result, we are now surrounded by screens. Sancho (2014) writes: "the audience gets excited and indignant, takes into their own hands the safeguarding of the public square just by looking and extending that visibility; they denounce the arbitrariness of the state by re-Tweeting what's going on by being vigilant, and therefore by demonstrating as an involved participant" (396).

As mentioned in the previous section, research on protest and the media reflects a preoccupation with Twitter, Facebook, Instagram, and other digital social media platforms, often assumed to be distinguishable from "old" media such as television and cinema (Mehan, Sennema and Tideman 2019; 2020). By connecting the screen with protest via "the public screen" and acknowledging the influential visual political discourse, DeLuca and Peeples (2002) argue that the most important public discussions take place via screens as the new modes of participation and perception which is in contract to the rational argument on which the Habermasian public sphere is founded. This particular nexus between culture and politics is where collective social action, individual identity, and symbolic activity meet (127). In better words, visual narratives offer the citizens to build their projects by sharing their experiences. They subvert communication practice as usual by occupying the medium and creating the message (Castells 2015, 9). The live broadcast feed from Tahrir Square, or Tehran or Kyiv can be defined as the instance of ordinary citizens, distant in space, but present in real-time, joining the occupied sites of protest around the world (van Ess 2017). Visual narrative is a strong tradition in studying social movements and how they place themselves in the world and history. According to Meyrowtiz (2009), narrative, protest, and television come together since they are sites of resistance and storytelling. Guertin and Buettner (2014) have referred to the Occupy Movement as an invitation to people "to intervene through direct action to tell their own stories" (378). Images, storytelling, and screen create as much as they represent reality; specific embodiments can condense the narrative into a single moment that stands for the entire event. They are in the nexus between culture and politics where collective social action, individual identity, and symbolic activity meet (DeLuca and Peeples. 2002, 133).

Comparing the television news in Athens in 2008, Tehran in 2009, and Cairo in 2011, Karin Baker (2019) asks whether the "visual icon" of protest represented in the top headlines and stories on four transnational news channels, Al Jazeera English (AJE), BBC World (BBCW), CNNI, and Russia Today (RT), and also among the winning entries in the World Press Photo competition (WPP). Focusing on Tehran's 2009 protests and following the announcement of the presidential protest, Baker (2019) stated: "Iranian authorities blocked websites and cell-phone transmissions, and foreign journalists were threatened, creating a near blackout for conventional news sources. As protests spread to other cities and countries with a large Iranian population, the color green, originally Mousavi's campaign color, was adopted as a symbol. The Green Movement continued to grow in the coming months, actively employing various media platforms despite government suppression and censorship" (131). In comparison with the television reports from Greece two years before, Baker (2019) highlighted the use of amateur images (and voices) in the television coverage points due to the lack of material from professional sources, which anchors these scenes in the minds and memories of the view in public (132). The World Press Photo (WPP) of the year was from the Italian Pietro Masturzo, who won the prestigious award with photographs of the rooftop protest in Tehran after dark, with roots in the 1979 Islamic Revolution. This prize-winning series of nine photographs of "rooftop protests" includes visual signs of daily life on the roofs of Tehran, which portray different protestors from those seen on television news (Baker 2019, 132).

In the case of the Tahrir Square protests, broadcast footage from the first days of the demonstrations included more examples of the faces and voices of protestors than in Tehran or Athens. The Square (Al-Meidan) is an intimate observational documentary on the political struggles and social unrests of the Egyptian Revolution through the protesters' eyes, through the life-changing journey, and through the euphoria of victory, uncertainties, revolution, and violence of the transitional period in Tahrir Square under military rule.

The Protest Movements during the COVID-19 Pandemic

The advent of the COVID-19 virus has been marked by various health, governmental, societal, and urban challenges. Inequalities have become more salient as poor people and minorities are more affected by the virus (Purkayastha 2020). The global pandemic confronted us with many contradictory and complex situations to rethink transformative about the kind of future we want for ourselves. The COVID-19 showed the lack of many national governments' effective response to the pandemic. However, the more action-oriented plan has been evident at the local and community level. The pandemic has stimulated a remarkable upswing in mutual aid, community activism, and caring behaviors' in response to both old and new challenges facing cities and communities (Hambleton 2020, 79).

To envision the Post-COVID urbanism and radical future, Hambleton (2020) asserts that "there can be no 'going back'; the future of society and the planet will not only be determined by national governments and international bodies but also by local government and strong place-based leadership" (20). The new civic leadership could be achieved by drawing the complementary strengths and knowledge of civil society, the state, the market, the co-creation, and the co-design of novel strategies to societal problems.

To make this happen, according to Hambleton (2020), the New Civic Leadership (NCL) has four key attributes: the urgent need to recognize and expand the power of place; the importance of activists and policymakers moving beyond "public" to embrace "civic" as a way of thinking; the urgency of switching attention from "management" to "leadership"; and, the essential task of co-creating far more innovative approaches to citizen participation and public problem-solving (20). Hambleton (2014) argues that by meaningfully empowering place leadership, local authorities can play a major role in expanding and enhancing the collective urban intelligence and giving power to local communities, offering them the leverages to tackle the spatial injustice and shape their post-pandemic future (91). They suggested new hybrid scenarios for social movements, protests, and social unrest. The social activities adapted to the circumstances determined by the social distancing and the impossibility of people gathering in physical spaces. Subsequently, from the start of the state of emergency, the people in different countries had various individual and collective responses to the support of health workers, systemic inequalities, loss of jobs, and other societal and financial challenges imposed by the governments. For example, in Hong Kong, seven thousand medical workers led a successful "epoch-making strike" as the new wave of union movements to take measures against the virus spread (Chan and Tsui 2020). In Spain, to reduce the reverse effects of COVID-19, the legacy of the 15M movement became a space for experimentation with new models based on feminism, the commons, DIY (Do It Yourself), anti-welfare, and anti-charity, which aimed to satisfy people's material needs at the same time as respecting, involving, and empowering them.

At the time of rising racial, social, and economic inequalities, the COVID-19 outbreak is an opportunity for humanity to a less unequal world. The social distancing makes the typical forms of protest impossible to carry out (Pleyers 2020, 295). Under social distancing, some state-led policies took advantage of social media to focus on the COVID-19 pandemic to silence social and political activities, censor criticism, and control the press (Zhang 2020). As Pleyers (2020) well-articulated, during the pandemic era, the movements for social justice have been particularly active, focusing on defending workers' rights, mutual aid and solidarity, monitoring policymakers, and popular education. These progressive movements combined the concrete practices and experiences to confront the reactionary, capitalist, and governmental actors that seek to shape and envision the world that would come out of it (296). Rather than disappearing, the social movements have adapted to the unexpected situations during the pandemic outbreak. In this sense, the pandemic broke the new global wave of protests. After the pandemic, the new radical practices have been generated to tackle the population's most urgent needs due to the lack of street activism in the squares and streets.

Major Findings

Significant upheavals have been manifested in the current years following the global financial crisis of 2008. The challenge of modern democracy has been how to join local participation with centralized global power. The nation-state has become too large to allow meaningful local involvement and citizen participation.

As an integral part of the protest spatialities, the insurgent cities are hosts to confront the democracy crisis across the globe. In this sense, the protest movements, social activism, grassroots practices for global change, and leaderless uprisings are come together in public space to echo their collective radical voice as the new form of decentralized government. The physical and the digital elements of a protest movements' hybrid reality make up the whole event. Focusing on visual narratives, the protest squares' representation on mainstream media such as television screens and cinema and the new digital media has been broad. The extensive use of digital technologies, including but not limited to social media platforms (such as Facebook, Twitter, and Instagram), digital mapping, e-petitions, and e-participation platforms, has been reshaping the protest movements around the world. Digital media and platforms have their challenges and deficiencies. Digital means and media are not unbiased for several reasons: first, media monopolization will cause discrimination of access to knowledge and data. Therefore, selected interpretations of facts, narratives, and events are expected. Second, the norms and values of the information receiver might not necessarily match the way the information is communicated and processed. Hence, such mismatch will result in misunderstandings, conflicts, and (dis)continuation of active participation.

The recent COVID-19 pandemic health crisis changed a lot of radical thinking on the issues we were dealing with before for a long time, such as existing inequalities, unjust distribution of resources, exclusivity, ethnical and racial segregation, isolation, and marginalization (Mehan 2021; Repellino, Martini and Mehan 2016). Following cultural and societal approaches in the study of progressive social movements, the pandemic period showed the importance of activism, resiliency, and solidarity in the daily life of the communities beyond the activists' circles.

Notes

1 See https://network.fearlesscities.com/ (Latest Accessed on 24 January 2022)
2 See https://www.commonsnetwork.org/what-we-do/ (Latest Accessed on 24 January 2022)
3 See https://www.right2city.org/(Latest Accessed on 24 January 2022)

References

Athrope, Caleb, and Martin Horak. 2021. "The End of the Right to the City: A Radical Cooperative View." *Urban Affairs Journal* 1–20.
Baker, K. 2019. "Icons of Protest in the Visual Cultures of News." In *Screening Protest: Visual Nattarives of Dissent Across Time, Space and Genre*, by Alexa Robertson, 121–149. London and New York: Routledge.
Barber, Benjamin R. 2013. *If Mayors Ruled the World: Dysfunctional Nations, Rising Cities*. New Haven: Yale University Press.
Bennett, W.L., and A. Segerberg. 2013. *The Logic of Connective Action: Digital Media and the Personalization of Contentious Politics*. Cambridge: Cambridge University Press.
Bookchin, Debbie. 2019. "The Future We Deserve." In *Fearless Cities: A Guide to the Global Municipalist Movement*, by Debbie Bookchin and Ada Colau. Oxford, UK: New Internationalist.
Brian, G. Smith, Rita Linjuan Men, and Reham Al-Sinan. 2015. "Tweeting Taksim communication power and social media advocacy in the Taksim square protests." *Computers in Human Behavior (Elsevier)* (50): 499–507.
Busquet, G. 2013. "Political Space in the Work of Henri Lefebvre: Ideology and Utopia." *Justice* 5: 1–12.
Caprotti, F. 2014. "Eco-Urbanism and the Eco-City, or, Denying the Right to the City?" *Antipode* 46: 1285–1303.

Casetti, F. 2013. "What Is a Screen Nowadays?" In *Public Space, Media Space*, by C. Berry, J. Harbord and R. Moore. Houndmills: Palgrave Macmillan.

Castells, Manuel. 2015. *Networks of Outrage and Hope: Social Movements in the Internet Age*. Cambridge; Malden, MA: Polity Press.

Chan, C., and A. Tsui. 2020. "Hong Kong: De Las Protestas Democr Ticas a La Huelga De Trabajadores M Dicos En La Pandemia." In *El Mundo En Suspenso. Pol tica y Movimiento En Tiempo De La Pandemia*, by B. Bringel and G. Pleyers, 152–159. Buenos Aires, Argentina: CLACSO.

Costanza-Chock, S. 2012. "Mic Check! Media Cultures and the Occupy Movement." *Social Movement Studies* 11 (3–4): 375–385.

DeLuca, K.M., and J. Peeples. 2002. "From Public Sphere to Public Screen: Democracy, Activism, and the "Violence" of Seattle." *Critical Studies in Media Communication* 19 (2): 125–151.

Frediani, Alexandre Aspen, and Rafaella Simas Lima. 2015. "Habitat III nATIONAL rePORTING processes: Locating the Right to the City and the Role of Civil Society." *The Bartlett Development Planning Unit*.

Frug, Gerald E., and David J. Barron. 2008. *City Bound: How States Stifle Urban Innovation*. Ithaca: Cornell University Press.

Gerbaudo, P. 2017. *Tweets and the Streets: Social media and Contemporary Activism*. London: Hurst & Company.

Glaeser, Edward. 2011. *Triumph of the City*. New York: Penguin.

Guertin, C., and A. Buettner. 2014. "Introduction: "We Are the Uninvited." *Convergence* 20 (4): 377–386.

Hambleton, Robin. 2014. *Leading the Inclusive City: Place-Based Innovation for a Bounded Planet*. Bristol: Policy Press.

—. 2020. *Cities and Communities Beyond COVID-19*. Bristol, UK: Bristol University Press.

Hou, Jeffrey. 2020. "Guerrilla Urbanism: Urban Design and the Practices of Resistance." *Urban Design International* (25): 117–125.

Kavada, A. 2015. "Creating the Collective: Social media, the Occupy Movement and Its Constitution as a Collective Actor." *Information, Communication & Society* 18 (8): 872–886.

Lefebvre, Henri. 2003. *The Urban Revolution*. Minnesota: University of Minnesota Press.

Lokot, Tetyana. 2021. *Beyond the Protest Square: Digital Media and Augmented Dissent*. London; New York: Rowman & Littlefield International.

Marx, K., and F. Engels. 2012. *The Communist Manifesto: A Modern Edition*. London: Verso.

Mattoni, Alice. 2020. "Making the Syntagma Square protests visible. Cultures of participation and activists' communication in Greek anti-austerity protests." *Information, Communication & Society* (Taylor and Francis) 23 (12): 1755–1769.

Mehan, A, H. Sennema, and S. Tideman. 2020. "Port City Heritage: Contested Pasts, Inclusive Futures?" *The Port City Futures Blog*. Leiden. Delft. Erasmus (LDE) Initiative.

Mehan, A. 2017. "Review of "The Empty Place: Democracy and Public Space" by Teresa Hoskyns." *ID: International Dialogue, A Multidisciplinary Journal of World Affairs* (University of Nebraska at Omaha (UNO)) 7: 86–90.

—. 2019. "Film About Cape Town Is Being Used to Raise Awareness, and to Ask Wider Questions." *The Conversation (Africa Pilot)* (Creative Common License) 1–7.

—. 2020. "The Port City's Cine-Scapes." *Port City Futures (PCF) Blog*. Leiden. Delft. Erasmus (LDE) Initative.

—. 2021. "EUKN Webinar 'Port Cities and Mega-Trends: Glocal Approaches to Sustainable Transitions'." *The Port City Futures Blog*. Leiden. Delft. Erasmus (LDE) Initiative.

Mehan, Asma, and Sina Mostafavi. 2022. "Building Resilient Communities Over Time." In *The Palgrave Encyclopedia of Urban and Regional Futures*, by Robert C. Brears. Cham, Switzerland: Palgrave Macmillan, Springer.

Mehan, Asma, and Bouchra Tafrata. 2022. "Embedding Justice in Climate Change Action." In *The Palgrave Encyclopedia of Urban and Regional Futures*, by Robert C. Brears. Cham, Switzerland: Palgrave Macmillan, Springer.

Meyrowitz, J. 2009. "We Liked to Watch: Television as Progenitor of the Surveillance Society." *The ANNALS of the American Academy of Political and Social Science* 625 (1): 32–48.

Panitch, L., and S. Gindin. 2013. *The Making of Global Capitalism: the Political Economy of American Empire*. London: Verso.

Pleyers, Geoffrey. 2020. "The Pandemic Is a Battlefield. Social Movements in the COVID-19 Lockdown." *Journal of Civil Society* 16 (4): 295–312.

Purcell, Mark. 2013. "The Right to the City: the Struggle for Democracy in the Urban Public Realm." *Policy and Politics* 43 (3): 311–327.

—. 2014. "Possible Worlds: Henri Lefebvre and the Right to the City." *Journal of Urban Affairs* 36 (1): 141–154.

Purkayastha, B. 2020. *Divided we stand- The pandemic in the US*. Open Movements – ISA 47 Open Democracy.

Repellino, Maria Paola, Laura Martini, and Asma Mehan. 2016. "Growing Environment Culture Through Urban Design Processes 城市设计促进环境文化." *NANFANG JIANZHU* 2: 67–73.

Robertson, Alexa. 2019. *Screening Protest: Visual Narratives of Dissent Across Time, Space and Genre*. London and New York: Taylor & Francis Group.

Sancho, G.R. 2014. "Networks, Insurgencies, and Prefigurative Politics: A Cycle of Global Indignation." *Covergence* 20 (4): 387–401.

Sassen, Saskia. 2001. *The Global City: New York, London, Tokyo*. Princeton: Princeton University Press.

Smith, J., and D. Wiest. 2012. *Social Movements in the World-System: The Politics of Crisis and Transformation*. New York: Russel Sage Foundation.

Soja, Edward W. 2010. *Seeking Spatial Justice*. Minneapolis: University of Minnesota Press.

Swyngedouw, Erik. 2018. *Promises of the Political: Insurgent Cities in a Post-Political Environment*. Cambridge: MIT Press.

Taylor, Dylan. 2017. *Social Movements and Democracy in the 21st Century.* Cham: Palgrave Macmillan.
Tenenboum-Weinblatt, K. 2014. "Producing Protest News: An Inquiry into Journalists' Narratives." *The International Journal of Press/Politics* 19 (4): 410–429.
van Ess, K. 2017. *The Future of Live.* Cambridge: Polity.
Zhang, J. 2020. "Implications De La Censura En China Durante La Crisis De La Covid-19." In *El Mundo En Suspenso*, by B. Bringel & G. Pleyers, 49–56. Buenos Aires, Argentina: CLASCO.

Epilogue

This chapter summarizes arguments from previous chapters to conceptualize the transitions from sacred to insurgent urbanism in Tehran. The book defined the city as the site of political choices, a dynamic palimpsest of socio-political inputs. Considering the city as a dynamic entity under constant transformation, formation, intervention, and deformation shows the transformative potential of modernization that creates, motivates, inspires, reverses, or intensifies a creative tension in urban form.

As discussed previously in Chapters 2 and 3, the structure of old Tehran (starting from the nineteenth century) was transformed dramatically by dominant modernization and urbanization strategies: the first one is the strategy of *Tabula Rasa* as a desire for sweeping renewal and methodological destruction that ultimately creates space for building new urban identity. As the result of *Tabula Rasa Planning* and *Haussmannization* of Tehran, the city transformed into an open matrix which led to or facilitated the production of active political space. Consequently, the built networks of streets and squares in the northern section of Tehran, like *the Toopkhaneh* and *Baharestan* squares, substituted the previous sacred and religious spaces such as Sepahsalar Mosque as the primary political public spaces of the city. These radical interventions started from the nationalization of the oil movement till the 1953 Iranian Coup d'état, which facilitated the formation of the bourgeois class into the Iranian society.

As a result, the new spatial segregated capital with two main streets, Shah-Reza (now Enghelab) and Pahlavi (now Vali-e Asr), formed the main East-West and North-South axes of the city's spatial structure. In addition, along the new East-West axis of the city, important institutions such as Tehran University were erected. As the result of these transformations, Tehran became a spatially segregated capital, traditionally defined by the *Mahallah* (quarter system) according to ethnoreligious divisions, not along class lines.

The concept of *Tabula Rasa* Planning provided the potential site for the construction of utopian dreams. As discussed extensively in Chapter 3, the second leading strategy of modernization in Tehran—*Utopian Urbanism*—is based on the revolutionary character of modern architecture that takes on a purely utopian dimension in the reintegration of city. The example of Tehran's Comprehensive Plan of 1968 (TCP 1968) defined the new East-West axis guided by a new superhighways network, which integrated all the elements of the 1960s' American City such as separation of functions, highways, suburbs, shopping malls, and dense housing areas. This new Master plan of Tehran envisaged a highly class-segregated and socially segregated society that spatially designed the loci of low-income and high-income citizens. However, the new residential quarters in the east-west axis of the capital became the primary location for middle-income residents of the city. Designing the *Ekbatan* Residential Complex on the western edge of Tehran and the new international Airport of the time—Mehrabad Airport—the grand-scale project of Shahyad (now Azadi) Square as the city's new gateway manifested the utopian nature of modern architecture as the results of Capitalist Values.

This Utopian urban vision expressed a desire for radical change that engaged directly with revolutionary relations. For designing the Shah's "Great Civilization" like Mussolini's "Olympiad of Civilization," Tehran became the site of ambitious and grandiose projects like *Shahestan Pahlavi* located in Abbas Abad hills. In the emerging metropolis, the new utopian projects like *Shahyad Square* became counter projects that provided an open space for revolutionaries. During the 1978–1979 Islamic Revolution of Iran, Enqelab Street and Azadi Square provided the primary geography of protest. The production of insurgent urbanism in Tehran results from utopian urbanism achieving its political status through semantic association depending on the collective memory of previous historical events. In this way, protestors re-appropriated the meaning of Azadi Square during the recent social movements.

Squares as Politics

Focusing on insurgent urbanism and the international experience of protest squares, the public space has been represented as the machine of disruption used by democrats against the authoritarian regime to disrupt forming an urban social network. This book defined the idea of "protest square" and "protest democracy" as a new global phenomenon in the process of revolutionary changes with distinctive urban characteristics such as centrality, strategic locus of governmental building, epidemic potential of revolutionary spirit, people-oriented participation, pre-existing historical and political memories, production of temporarily just urban spaces, locus of mass transportation networks, spatial flexibility, and monumentality. Due to the liminal feature of the spatialities of revolution, one normal end but a new, stable normal has not emerged yet. As a result, insurgent spaces like protest squares shape and define the transformative experience of revolutions as liminal spaces. The case of Azadi Square in Tehran as a prestigious project by the shah that became anti-project after the Islamic Revolution is proof of this claim. Rather than being destroyed, it continues to be a significant focal point for gatherings, protests, and social unrest, including the massive demonstrations of the so-called Green Movement in the aftermath of the 2009 Presidential elections.

Using Turner's three-stage ritual process (*antistructure*, *liminal*, and *communitas*) in the case of protest squares can theorize the transformative processes of insurgent urbanism during the political revolutions and social movements. In the first place, protest squares became *antistructure* (in Turner's Term), in which most of the characteristics that defined the normal configuration of socio-political life ceased to function. In the second step, the *liminal* is where few or none of the attributes of the past have been left. The final stage, *Comunitas*, is settling back into a new social structure with the intense feeling of community and solidarity experienced by those who broke down the social statuses. This epidemic sense of solidarity heralds the protest squares' political message to inspire other movements worldwide.

The experiences of the recent occupy movements and protest squares stress the global demand for participatory democracy for legitimate social conflict. To approach the space of participatory democracy, which introduces the people as both legitimizing the government and being represented, we need to create "an empty place of power." In other words, in this democratic space, people are sources of power, but it is the power of nobody, so, no figure can embody society's unity. This openness or nonidentical feature of "empty place of power," is the same feature in protest squares and insurgent urbanism during the social movements and political revolutions. That is to say, democracies should have empty centers.

For better understanding of this ongoing struggle for achieving real democracy around the world, which represented the democracy as the struggle for democracy rather than a utopian stable and universal

Epilogue 111

condition, the concept of "Rhizomatic Politics" by *Deleuze* and *Guttari* has been studied. The idea of *becoming democrat*, instead of *being democratic*, is the criticism of the present democracy and searching for the new "configuration." For fulfilling the idea of becoming democrat, the Lefebvre's "urban society" or Deleuzian "open society" is never stable, always open to the future, always resisting the forces that repress and impede "the whole of freedom." This definition of unstable "open society" in "Rhizomatic Politics" connected the processes of "becoming democratic" and "becoming revolutionary"; a becoming that is always underway. For resisting what is intolerable in the present and achieve the open society, we need the "people to come" who "have the chance to invent themselves."

For a better understanding of this ongoing struggle for achieving real democracy around the world, which represented democracy as the struggle for democracy rather than a utopian stable and universal condition, the concept of "Rhizomatic Politics" by *Deleuze* and *Guattari* has been studied. The idea of *becoming a democrat*, instead of *being democratic*, is the criticism of the present democracy and searching for a new "configuration." For fulfilling the idea of becoming a democrat, Lefebvre's "urban society" or Deleuzian's "open society" is never stable, always open to the future, always resisting the forces that repress and impede "the whole of freedom." This definition of unstable "open society" in "Rhizomatic Politics" connected the processes of "becoming democratic" and "becoming revolutionary"; a becoming that is always underway. To resist what is intolerable in the present and achieve an open society, we need the "people to come" who "have the chance to invent themselves."

Deluze and *Guttari's* imagery of rhizomes in defining the idea of a body (politics) without organs (party) introduces revolutionary groups whose members engage each other in horizontal and non-hierarchical relations. *Tahrir Square* in *Cairo*, *Puerta del Sol* in *Madrid*, *Azadi Square* in Tehran, and *Taksim Square* in *Istanbul* were collections of individuals with organ-less and center-less leadership. In this new definition, the new global and radical urban social movements like "Take the Square," "Fearless Cities," or "The Global Platform for the Right to the City (GPR2C)" movements can be defined as an ongoing struggle of becoming democratic and revolutionary in approaching the possible open society.

The new digital technologies altered the dynamics of protest movements in all kinds of states. In Chapter 5, the role of digital agency in sustaining the protest movements has been analyzed. Through going through the various case studies of recent protest squares such

112 Epilogue

as Athens in 2008, Tehran in 2009, and Cairo in 2011, the extensive use and the critical role of both old media, such as television reports, cinema, and visual screens, as well as the digital platforms, such as Twitter, websites, blogs, Instagram, Twitter, e-petitions, and digital mapping, have been discussed.

The recent COVID-19 pandemic introduced innovative and unexpected ways of hybrid movements and protested democracy across the globe. The racial inequalities, spatial segregations, authoritarianism, blocking of migratory movements, and pressure to restrict women's rights are becoming a significant focus in COVID-19 circumstances. Moving most activity online during COVID-19 has resulted in virtual online protests and hybridity as the self-imposing alternatives. Under the pandemic conditions, creating alternative (urban) systems appear as bottom-up solidarity, micro-networks, and voluntary action, such as teaching aids, neighborhood shopping offers, meal delivery for the public, and local fundraisers for medical equipment. To envision the radical protest movements after the COVID-19 pandemic, it is essential to analyze the various online protests, offline activism, and street protest tactics in the use of space, which will finally attract substantially higher levels of media attention.

Index

Note: **Bold** page numbers refer to tables and *italic* page numbers refer to figures.

Achaemenid inscriptions 16
action-oriented plan 101–102
actor-network theory (ANT) 28
Afsharnaderi, Kamran 17
Agora of Smyrna 11
Ali, Imam 20
Ali Qapu Palace 20–21
Al Jazeera English (AJE) 100–101
Al-Sinan, Reham 99
Amsterdam and Brussels-based Common Network 96
Anglophones 99
anti-government demonstrations 88
antistructure 77–78, 89, 110
Arabic-Persian period 12–13
architecture: contemporary histography 2; democratic values 1; modern 70–71; paradigms 54; politics in 1; revolution 55–56; theory 1; traditions on 1; urbanism 3–5; utopian nature of 56–59
Architecture from the Outside (Grosz) 2
Arendt, Hannah: *On Revolution* 78
Aristotle 92
Arnold, Dana 2
Avery, Peter 69–70
Azadi Square 86–88, 110
Azimi, Fakhreddin: *Quest for Democracy in Iran* 69–70

Babylon 20
Baghdad 14–15

Baharestan squares 108
Baker, Karin 100–101
Baladieh 39
banlieue 30
Barron, David J. 92
Barthes, Roland: *Empire of Signs* 7
Basson, Steve 2
Bayat, Asef 34, 36
BBC World (BBCW) 100–101
Bennett, W.L. 98–99
Berman, Marshall 31
Black Lives Matter movement 93
"blank slate"/"blank canvas" 8
Bookchin, Murray 2; *The Rise and Decline of Citizenship* 10–11
"bottom-up" forms of violence 76
Boyer, M. Christine 68
Breaking Boundaries (Wylda) 78–79
Brian, G. 99
Bristol 93
Broadacre City/"Living City" 59
Brott, Simone 55
Buettner, A. 100
Buhler, General Alexander 32
built environment 3
Buzarjomehri, Karim Agha Khan 43

Calvino, Italo: *Invisible Cities* 84
capitalist model 70
Casetti, F. 100
Castells, Manuel 98
"catching-up" narratives 36

Cerdà, Ildefonso 29–30
Chahar Bagh Avenue 22
Chaleh Meydan 36
circuits of knowledge 28
The City Squares (Webb) 8, 9
CNNI 100–101
Coleman, Nathaniel 56
Colston, Edward 93
comitia tributa 11
communication space 8
comunitas 78, 89, 110
Constitutional Revolution 35
"constructive potency" 68–69
contextualization 47
"contextualized" spatial language 26
cosmopolitanism 94
Costanza-Chock, S. 98
Courtyard 17
COVID-19 pandemic 5, 101–103, 104, 112
"creative destruction" 31
"cultural repertoires" 4
Curzon, George 33–34

decontextualization 47
De Landa, Manuel 82
Deleuze, Gilles 77, 81–82, 89, 111; *Le Bergsonisme* 83–84
Democracia Real Ya (Real Democracy Now) 95
democracy 3; crisis 92; Deleuze and Guattari's views 83; success of cities 92–93
De Romeiser, François 39
"die Paradiesische Stadt" 20
digital technologies 111–112
discourse analysis 28
Doxiadis Associates 66
Dubrulle, Roland Marcel 43–44

East-West axis 109
Ecole des Beaux-Arts 62
Ekbatan Residential Complex 63, 65, 109
Empire of Signs (Barthes) 7
The "Empty Place of Power" 79–81, 110
"Enforced Mobility" 59
Enqelab Square 86–88
Ērānšahr 12–13, 15–16

Euromaidan protest 84
European Renaissance 19
"exporter" and "importer" of planning 28
Exposition Universelle de (1876) 30–31

Farabi, Islamic Philosopher 16
Fearless Cities/Cities of Change 95–96
Ferguson, Priscilla Parkhurst 30
Flynn, Bernard 80
Fora Civilica 11
Fora Venalia 11
Ford Foundation 62
Foucault, Michel 2, 18, 54, 68–69
Freedom Square 70, 88–89
French Revolution 57
Friedmann, John 47
Frug, Gerald E. 92

Gaube, Heinz 14
Ghaffari, Fereydun 62
"Gilet-Jaunes" uprisings 93
"Girls of Revolution Street" 88
Glaeser, Edward 92
global capitalism 97
The Global Municipalism Movement 95–96
Global Platform for the Right to the City (GRP2C) 96–98, 111
Global South 3–5
Godard, André 43–44
Grassroots reactions 93
Greco-Mesopotamian style 13
Greek Agora 10–11
Green Movement 101, 110
Grigor, Talinn 66, 69
Grosz, Elizabeth 54; *Architecture from the Outside* 2
Gruen, Victor 57–58, 63
Guattari, Félix 77, 81–82, 83, 89, 111
Guertin, C. 100
Gurney, John 34

Habermas, Jurgen 69
Hambleton, Robin 102
Haussmann, Georges-Eugène 29–30, 34, 45
Haussmannization 108

Healy, Patsy 28, 44
hegemonic cityscapes 86
Helmer, Stephen D. 31
Henry, James 35
Herbert, Thomas 20, 21
Herzfeld, Ernst 35
heterotopia 54, 68–70
Heynen, Hilde 57
High Economic Council (1937) 37
hiroba 8
Hong Kong 102
horse-racing ground 12
Hosseiniyes 19
Hou, Jeffery 92
Housing and Sustainable Development (Habitat III) 96
Howard, Ebenezer 57, 59
Human Settlements Conference (Habitat II) 96
hybrid multiplicity 99

ideological symbolism 84–86
Image and Pilgrimage in Christian Culture (Turner) 77
"in-between" spaces 78
"inside-out" spaces 78
insurgent cities: COVID-19 pandemic, protest movements 101–103, 104; Fearless Cities 95–96; Global Platform for the Right to the City 96–98; screening dissent 99–100; social media protests 98–99; "Take the Square" movement 94–95
insurgent urbanism 76, 77, 86, 89, 108–110
intrinsic logic (Eigenlogik) 3–4
Invisible Cities (Calvino) 84
"Involuntary Mobility" 59
Iran: British colonial city 36–37; cities 13–14; country's resources, exploitation of 34–35; Meidan 9–15, *10*, *13*, 22–23; paradise 15–17; street-widening act (1933) 39–44, *40*, **41–42**; urbanism 5; *see also* Tehran
Iranian/Middle Eastern Urbanism. 5
Isfahan (1598–1722 AD) 20
Islamic Revolution 86–88, 110
Italian piazza square/marketplace 12

Jacobs, Jane 59
Jameson, Fredric 55
Jan, Wilem Duyvendak 29
Japan: public spaces 7–8; sacred space 8
Jinnai, Hidenobu: *Tokyo: A Spatial Anthropology* 8

Kahn, Louis 66–67
Kanda, Shun 8
Katouzian, Homa 43
Kavada, A. 98
Kennedy Administration 61–62
Khan, Sadiq 93
King, Anthony D. 28–29
Kircher, Athanasius 15
Kostof, Spiro 34
Kozlowski, Marek 83
Kroeber, Karl 54
"Kuala Lumpur: Community, Infrastructure, and Urban Inclusivity" (Kozlowski, Mehan and Nawratek) 83

La Ville Radiuse (The Radiant City) (Le Corbusier) 31
Leach, Neil 55
Le Corbusier 31, 53, 58, *Vers une architecture* 55–56
Le Droit à la ville (Lefebvre) 96–97
Lefebvre, Henri 76, 81, 89, 111; *Le Droit à la ville* 96–97; *Urban Revolution* 82, 83
Lefort, Claude 79–80
Lehrman, Jonas Benzion 17
liberation municipalism 96
Lieto, Laura 47
limen 78
liminal 89, 110
liminality 77–79
"Liminality, Revolutions, and Protest Squares" 77
Lockhart, Lawrence 20

Madrid (AcampadaSol) 95
Mahalleh system 34, 46, 109
Maidan/ майдан 9
"The Many Mirrors of Foucault and Their Architectural Reflections" (Boyer) 68

Masturzo, Pietro 101
Matin-Asgari 36–37
Mattoni, Alice 99
Mazdaean-Zoroastrian ideology 16
McFarlane, Colin 29
Mehan, Asma 83
Meidan 9–15, *10, 13*, 22–23
Meidan-e Naqsh-e Jahan *21*, 21–22
Men, Rita Linjuan 99
"Metropolis of Tomorrow" 57–58, 59–67, *60, 61, 63, 64, 65, 67*
Meyrowtiz, J. 100
micro-powers 2–3
Middle Eastern: cities 4; urbanism 5
Milani, Abbas 34
Mission for my Country (Reza Shah) 64–66
modern history 3
modernity 1
"modernization myth" 28
modern urban planning 27–28
Moharram 19
Mozaffari, Ali 65
Mumford, Lewis 59

National Center of Tehran 66–67
Nawratek, Krzysztof 83
neoliberalism 94
New Civic Leadership (NCL) 102
'Newspeak' 2
Nikpei, Gholam Reza 62

Occupy Wall Street Movement (2011) 93, 93, 98, 100
Oku 8
Oldfield, Sophie 4
On Revolution (Arendt) 78
Orange Revolution 84
"Oriental cities" 14
Orwell, George 2
Oxford Dictionary of Architecture 9

Pahlavi regime 66; *see also* Reza Shah Pahlavi, Mohammad
παραδεισος *[paradeisos]* 15
paradise 15–17
paridayda 15
Paris 26; Haussmann's interventions 29–31; modernization 29–30
Parnell, Susan 4

Persepolis/Parse 13–14, 20
Persian Empire 86
Perso-Shi'i imperial ideology 19
Peterson, Mark Allen 79
Piazza di San Marco 21
Picon, Antoine 56
Pleyers, G. 103
Pnyx 11
political agency 97
political experiences 80
The Political Locus of Sovereignty 17–22
political philosophy 3
Pope Sixtus V 22
"postmodernity" 68–69
power struggles 1
primary interpretive scheme 47
"processual" ritual analysis 79
protest democracy 110
protest square 110
public spaces 1; Japan 7–8
Purcell, Mark 82

Qajar monarchs 36
quarter system 34
quattrocento/schermo 99
Quest for Democracy in Iran (Azimi) 69–70

Rabbat, Nasser 14
radical urbanism: conceptualizing 76–77; "empty place of power" 79–81; liminality 77–79, 88; protest squares 84–88; "rhizomatic" democracy 81–84; social movements 81–84
Rajchman, John 54
Ramadan 19
recontextualization 47
"relative comparative approach" 29
Republican Turkey 36–37
resource distribution 97
revolutionary experiences 80–81
Reza Shah Pahlavi, Mohammad 35–36, 37, 43, 86; *Mission for my Country* 64–66
rhizomatic democracy 81–84
"Rhizomatic Politics" 111
"Rhodes must fall" campaign 93
Right to the City (R2C) 96–97

Index 117

The Rise and Decline of Citizenship (Bookchin) 10–11
Ritter, Carl 20
Robertson, Alexa 99
Robertson, Jaquelin T. 67
Robinson, Jennifer 29
Russian invasion, Ukraine 9
Russia Today (RT) 100–101

sacred space 8
Safavid dynasty (1501–1736 AC) 19–20
Safavid Shah Abbas I. 22
Sassanid Empire 12, 15
Sassen, Saskia 93
"screen explosion" 100
screening dissent 99–100
Second World War 93
Segerberg, A. 98–99
Seleucid Empire (312–364 BC) 13
Sepahsalar Mosque 108
Shahestan Pahlavi 109
Shahri, Jafar 43
Shahyad monument 69
Shahyad Square 64, 70, 86
Shakibi, Zhand 69–70
Sheikh Lotf-Allah Chapel-Mosque 21
Shāhnāmeh of Ferdowsī, King Khusrow 15–16
Siroux, Maxime 43–44
Smith, Jackie 94
social change 97
social distancing 102–103
social justice 97
social media 93, 98–99, 100, 103
social movements 76, 81–84, 94, 102
socio-cultural diversity 97
socio-structural constraints 77
Soja, Edward 68, 97
southern urbanism scholarship 4
sovereignty 17–22
spatial narrative style 54
"spatial turn" 68–69
Squares: digital era 98–99; politics 109–112; as politics 84–88, *85*; Webb's views 8, 9
state of emergency 102
"Statues must fall" campaigns 93
Stoa 11

street-widening act (1933) 39–44, *40*, **41–42**
Sustainable Development Goals (SDGs) 5
Swyngedouw, Erik 93–94
Syntagma Square 99

Tabula Rasa 108, 109
Tafuri, Manfredo 56
Tahrir Square 79, 101
Take the Square and Right to the City (RTTC) 94
"Take the Square" movement 94–95
Taksim Square 99, 111
Tange, Kenzo 8, 66–67
Tehran: Action Plan 66; global urban dilemmas 5; master plan 62, *63*; Master plan 109; mayors 41, 43; modernization 31–34, *32, 33*; morphological analysis 34–35; National Center of Tehran 66–67; new avenues *45*; newly built streets **41–42**; planning schemes 53; segregated capital 108–109; social fabric 34; socio-political life 26–27; street layout plan *40*; street map 26–27; structure of 108; transformations 4–5; urban form 26–27; urban planning 53; *see also* Iran
Tehran's Comprehensive Plan (TCP) 109
Tekkiyes 19
Temple Mount of *Jerusalem* 9
Teoria General de la urbanización (Cerdà) 29–30
"Third World" 70
Tiananmen Square 9, 21
Tobacco Protest (1981) 36
Tokyo: A Spatial Anthropology (Jinnai) 8
Toopkhaneh squares 108
totalitarianism 80
totalizing statepower 54
"Towards a New Architecture" (Corbusier) 53
transformative dynamism 1
transformative power 77, 78–79
trans-Iranian railway project 39

118 *Index*

"transnational planning transfer" discipline 27, 28–29, 47
Turco-Iranian urban forms 19
Turkey: First Five-year Plan 37
Turner, Edith 77–78
Turner, Victor 77–78, 79
Twelve Shi'ism 19

Ukraine, Russian invasion 9
universal capitalism 81–82
urban agendas 95–96
urban analysis 3
Urban Development and Renewal Act 62
Urbaniste-Ingenieur des Travaux Publics (Public Works Engineer) 44
urbanization myth 34–39, *35*, *37*, *38*
Urban Revolution (Lefebvre) 82, 83
urban society 82–83, 89
urban spaces 76
utopian architecture 56–59
Utopian Urbanism 109

Vers une architecture (Le Corbusier) 55–56
Vilder, Anthony 58

Ville Radieuse (Radiant City or Machine City) 58
visual narratives 100, 103

Wakeman, Rosemary 59
Ward, Tory 28, 29
Webb, Michael: *The City Squares* 8, 9
What is Philosophy? (Deleuze and Guattari) 81–82
"White Revolution"/"Revolution of Shah and People," 62
Wiest, Dawn 94
Wirth, Eugen 14
World Press Photo competition (WPP) 101
Wright, Frank Lloyd 59
Wylda, Harald: *Breaking Boundaries* 78–79

Yang, Guobin 78
Yes We Camp 95

Zayanderud River 22
Zevi, Bruno 56
Zoroastrian religion 12

For Product Safety Concerns and Information please contact our EU
representative GPSR@taylorandfrancis.com
Taylor & Francis Verlag GmbH, Kaufingerstraße 24, 80331 München, Germany

www.ingramcontent.com/pod-product-compliance
Lightning Source LLC
Chambersburg PA
CBHW051754230426
43670CB00012B/2276